Presumed Guilty:

The Prosecution of The Vaughn 17

ARIA ORCHARD

Presumed Guilty

The Prosecution of The Vaughn 17

by

Aria Orchard

Bella Amina Publishing- Mt. Dora

The contents of this publication is a work of non-fiction. The names and events in this book are true. Direct quotes are used wherever possible. Court records, victim statements, and eyewitness accounts are documented within the texts of this book.

Names: Orchard, Aria, - author
Description: First Edition: a non-fiction novel, Florida
ISBN : 979-8-88796-481-2

Bella Amina Publishing- Mt. Dora

For Dalton

FORWARD

On February 1, 2017, inmates at the James T Vaughn Correctional Center in Smyrna, Delaware took control of the C Building at the facility. In Wednesday's early morning hours, the storm that had been brewing for decades finally erupted.

Four members of the Department of Corrections staff were taken hostage; prison counselor Patricia May, guards Joshua Wilkinson and Winslow Smith, and Sgt. Steven Floyd.

As the police attempted to regain control of the building, prison guards fought for their lives inside, uninvolved inmates tried to find safety, and the entire world watched helplessly as the tragedy unfolded. Reporters, police officers, protestors, and community members lined the streets outside the prison walls.

In the end, Patricia May was released unharmed after being protected by inmates. Both Wilkinson and Smith, as well as Sgt Floyd, were severely beaten during the nearly twenty-hour siege. The guards were ultimately released, but Sgt. Floyd succumbed to his injuries.

Vaughn Prison is regarded as a maximum security prison but, surprisingly, it did not have any cameras installed in the building. To piece together what actually happened that day, investigators needed to rely on the testimony of witnesses and the statements of inmates.

It was evident that this task was easy since one of the prisoners, Royal Downs, approached investigators the day after the riot and implicated several of the inmates responsible for the uprising.

Consequently, seventeen men were swiftly indicted for their alleged role in the uprising. Each man indicted on a slew of charges, including rioting, kidnapping, and murder of Sgt. Steven Floyd.

This book explores in detail the history of the trouble at the prison, the story as it unfolded from the perspective of the hostages and eyewitnesses, and the fate of the seventeen prisoners before, during, and after their trials.

There are several important aspects of this story, including exposing a broken judicial system, an ineffective rehabilitation program, and inconsistent policies that contributed to the uprising.

Chapter 1

James T Vaughn Correctional Center is a Level 5 prison facility for men, making it one of the largest in Delaware. It is the largest of the state's adult male prisons. Approximately 2,500 inmates are housed in this facility, which includes minimum, medium, and maximum-level offenders. It is here that men who have been sentenced to death await their final judgment.

Vaughn is the location where executions are conducted. In 1971, the prison was opened with a capacity of 441. Since then, the facility has been expanded to accommodate more than 2,600 men. Construction began in 1996, adding 888 additional beds to the facility. The expansion included the construction of 600 new maximum security cells, fencing, 6 miles of razor wire, as well as a new central and perimeter tower.

A total of six new housing units have been constructed for the cells. Three hundred of the cells have one bed, whereas the remainder have two beds, unless they are handicap-accessible, in which case they have a single bed. Among the new additions are the Security Housing Unit (SHU) and the Medium-High Housing Unit (MHU).

In essence, within this Building Unit. A total of 300 cells are located in the SHU. Each cell consists of one bunk. Inmates are restricted in their access to visitations, telephone calls, and the number of personal items they may keep in their cells.

Those who are not sentenced to death may be able to earn the right to be released from the Special Housing Unit (SHU) by displaying appropriate behavior, obeying institutional rules, and participating in treatment, education, and/or work programs.

Currently, there are no programs to provide treatment, education, or employment. There is a lack of consistency in policies, and inmates located in the SHU building are essentially confined to the building without any motivation or purpose.

Compared to the SHU, the MHU is a step lower, and compared to the general population, it is a step higher. There are more privileges for inmates in the MHU than inmates in the SHU, but fewer privileges for inmates in the general population. Five hundred and eighty-eight beds are available in 300 cells in the MHU.

The allegations of abuse, mistreatment, and torture committed by staff have been well-known to both inmates and employees over the years. Some employees have expressed concerns about the maltreatment of inmates, including excessive use of force, denying medical care for serious illnesses, and prolonged solitary confinement (which sometimes lasted years).

Jake Fox, a former DOC inmate, was awarded $65, 000 in April of 2019. Corporal Eben Boyce was found to have committed assault and battery and violated Jake Fox's constitutional right against cruel and unusual punishment by the jury.

In the complaint, Fox stated that he looked inside another holding cell while passing it in order to determine whether he recognized anyone. In response, Boyce immediately charged Mr. Fox, screaming *"What the fuck did you say, boy?"*

He then grabbed Fox by his shirt, lifted him off the ground, and slammed him against the concrete. When Fox was down, he continued to forcefully slam his head against the cement for several minutes.

Throughout this vicious attack, Mr. Fox was confined in leg shackles and handcuffs. Dazed and disoriented, Fox's hearing was postponed. A total of nine stitches were required to close the wound.

In the end, no discipline was imposed on the Officer, or he was criminally charged. Boyce was actually promoted to the rank of Lieutenant.

This case is particularly noteworthy since prisoner lawsuits are generally dismissed or settled. Generally, people believe that an inmate who is currently incarcerated lacks credibility. Mr. Fox was fortunate in that the jury was able to disregard his criminal background and do what was right in this case.

It has been reported that there have been several lawsuits in which Gov. John Carney, Delaware's Governor, has been named as a defendant.

The civil suits assert that elected officials with oversight of the DOC, including governors, have ignored all of the complaints and that the Department of Corrections has simply been warehousing inmates, allowing correctional officers to abuse them, and providing very little rehabilitation or education to them.

Unfortunately, those lawsuits have not resulted in a significant improvement in inmate treatment.

The last major hostage situation in Delaware occurred in 2004, when an inmate took a female counselor hostage, raped her, and was eventually shot dead after nearly seven hours of hostage negotiations.

Critics contend that state leadership ignored problems at Vaughn, which contributed to the attack and failed to implement measures to calm tensions inside the four prisons in the state and prevent the 2017 riots.

Chapter 2

The feeling of dread that Patricia May felt when she reported for work on that particular day was palpable. Her feeling was not a new one, as she had been assigned to building C for a number of years and had felt it every single day since then.

A former probation and parole officer before becoming a counselor, May holds a degree in criminology and has extensive experience working with individuals with criminal backgrounds. She is accustomed to working with individuals who have criminal records. Building C, however, suffered from not just the most violent offenders but was also overcrowded and understaffed in that particular building.

The facility was plagued by mismanagement, poor communication, a culture of negativity, and adversarial relationships among staff, administrators, and inmates. It was in desperate need of a better living environment, counseling, and programs to help the inmates rehabilitate themselves.

According to her, inmates are being held in prisons for "far too long" and if correctional officials are thinking about how they should be treated they are antiquated in their thinking.

There were also no programs that were geared toward rehabilitation and reintegration into society. Building C was more of a housing holding area whose only purpose was to shelter bodies.

"It was common knowledge that the riot was going to come about," she added. *"We just didn't know when".*

In the moments before the riot broke out, she had received permission from Sgt. Steven Floyd to have an inmate visit her office. About 30 minutes into the meeting, another prisoner burst into the meeting with a sharp weapon.

"He said, 'Ms. May, I don't want to hurt you, but if you don't do everything I tell you, I'm going to have to stab you,'" she said.

As far as she could tell, it wasn't a shank knife or homemade knife; it appeared to be a commercial knife instead. The inmate with whom she was meeting ran out of the room immediately, leaving her alone with the armed man.

Even though he did not wear a mask, she was unable to identify him. As she remembered, he was an older man, perhaps between 30 and 40 years of age, and he was taller than her, it appears 5'4 - to 6' tall. A black man of average build and medium to dark complexion.

She was given a list of phone numbers by the knife-wielding inmate for her to contact. One was to The News Journal, a local newspaper in

New Castle, Delaware. There is a special code that needs to be entered to make outbound calls at the facility. Because May was frightened, she did not move fast enough for the inmate, and he was becoming increasingly frustrated as a result. The inmate took the phone from Counselor May and attempted the calls himself.

She had already deliberately knocked the phone off the hook in an attempt to elicit a response from someone, unbeknownst to the inmate. There was a hope that somewhere, someone would notice that the phone was off the hook and may realize that something was wrong.

After struggling with how to make a phone call, the inmate told her to send an email to the News Journal, where he took the mouse from her, but again, he was unable to figure out how to use it.

He began the process of immobilizing her, by binding her hands and feet to the chair. A hood was then placed over her head, blocking off her view of anything around her, and her hands and feet were soon tied to ensure she would not be able to move.

Outside her door, she could hear the violence taking place. The inmates ransacked the building, set fire to it, and barricaded its entrances.

A short while later, she was led from the office and had no view of anything other than the ground. As she remembered, the hood seemed to be well-made as if it had taken some time to make, as if it had taken some skill to construct.

Her head was down, and she could hear a fight going on in the hallway. The woman walked down the hall not being able to see in front of her, but she noticed a considerable amount of blood on the ground as she moved along. There was blood everywhere.

She found herself in a room seated on an odd metal object with a bed nearby. She thought to herself that perhaps the room might be a cell.

The noise that surrounded her was deafening. Her memories of the attack are filled with the sounds of metal being thrown and voices yelling as a result of the attack. She had no idea what was going to happen to her and was completely terrified and frightened beyond belief.

As a devout Christian, Patricia prayed to God, asking Him to keep her safe, and when it came time for her to die on that day, she prayed to welcome her home.

At one point, a cell phone was placed to her ear, and she heard a female voice on the other end say, *"I'm Michael's mom, they say you're gonna be OK."*

In a momentary sense of relief, she felt as if GOD had heard her prayers and had given her a reply.

There was a man who periodically checked on her to make sure she was doing well. Upon hearing the voice, she recognized it as Victor Graham, an inmate in the prison.

Her memory of how long she had spent there was somewhat foggy since the ordeal seemed surreal to her at the time.

The removal of Mrs. May to a different cell took place after somebody knocked on the window and people outside were thought to know where she was and where she was located.

The hood was removed from her head, and she was placed in another cell without her hood. As the room fell completely into darkness, blackness enveloped the room as it became pitch dark. It was only after the inmate shut the cell doors that she saw three men inside. Her eyes adjusted to the dim lighting as the inmate shut the doors.

As one of the men explained, it would be safer for them if 'they came in shooting'.

The thought of Attica immediately came into Patricia's mind at that moment.

She sat alone in the cell with the three men, each of whom had written their names on a piece of paper and given it to her to read. It was important to them that people knew who they were. While she remembered Trey Downing and Michael Carrillo's names, she hadn't recalled the name of the third man.

After the interview was conducted, it was revealed that the men mentioned were Donald Parkell and Anthony Morrow. Mrs. May had obviously been confused and does not recall where the names she initially mentioned came from.

In her words, Mrs. May said that they protected her and treated her with kindness. During the interview, she recalled that she was offered headache medication, food, and water.

When one of the inmates asked her what kind of music she preferred, she was able to reply that her favorite type of music was Christian rock.

When he went to retrieve the radio, he was unable to receive any reception at all. It was the same inmate who stated he was a "New Christian" and sang to her.

To comfort her, Morrow looked for his Bible and sat down with her to read scriptures from it. The two of them began talking about life and having faith in God. Mrs. May held the Bible close to her chest. It made her feel safe.

Instead of forcing her to go to the lavatory located in the cell when she needed to use it, the men had taken her to the staff toilet twice.

The first time she went to the bathroom, she was carried in a chair over the debris in the hallway, however, on the second trip, it had been removed for her, and she was provided toilet paper, and water to wash her hands with because the water had been cut off.

Mrs. May recalls Anthony Morrow telling her that they were also hostages as well. *"We didn't want any part of it,"* He said.

Although it was clear that the inmates she was in the company of had no control over what happened to her, she requested that if any of the other hostages were injured, they be released first.

It was 3 am when CERT (Correctional Emergency Response Team) gained entry into the prison. In order to ensure that she would be the one to be seen first, Mrs. May stood by the window.

She could hear the inmates screaming, *"Counselor, come down here!"* as CERT entered the tier in the prison.

It was the inmates that led CERT to the location of where the panel was located to unlock the cell. As soon as they removed Ms. May from the building, she was outside in fewer than two minutes.

She did not recall what happened to the three inmates she was locked in the cell with.

Aria Orchard

Chapter 3

Sgt. Steven Floyd was in the yard when a fight broke out between two inmates. In order to intervene, he called it in on his radio and tried to get involved. He had no idea that the fight was part of a pre-planned plot that was to be used as the catalyst for the uprising.

There was only Floyd in the yard that day, and several inmates quickly came swarming around him. Majority of the inmates attacking Floyd that day wore masks to conceal their identity. But, there were other's that didn't bother.

Perhaps, they wanted Floyd to see who they were. As he was rushed inside of the building, he was hit with fire extinguisher, as well as homemade weapons. One inmate describes what he witnessed that morning. He asked only to be referred to as 'Andy'.

"You hear a lot of thumping, and it's really heavy and intense...normally you don't just go look at what's going on. I pretty much mind my business a lot, but this particular morning I heard the noise of like desks being--boom, boom, blam, blam!" Andy described.

"I heard Floyd--Sgt. [Steven] Floyd--say, 'Code 1, Code 1, Code 1.' He said it three times. I said, 'Man, this guy's playing,' 'cause normally he jokes around a lot. This morning it wasn't no joke because...he said it again, and you heard the noise. I gets up and I come out my cell and I looked from my cell door and I see the scuffle."

Andy recalled that he saw three inmates attacking Floyd and tried to get his hands behind his back. He also saw that only two of the men were wearing masks. He heard Floyd say, *"Why are you doing this? I know who you are."*

Visually upset, Andy clears his throat and continues describing what he witnessed that horrible morning.

"I see one inmate...he looked like he had something in his hand, and he was hitting him in the neck area...and I seen blood and thought, 'Oh this is real!' At one point, it was constantly, they was on him. It was intense, it was intense.

His hand was moving so fast, I knew he had to have an object in his hand because every time he was hitting him it was so fast, and he was hitting him with a vigor, and you could see blood, but I didn't see what kind of object he had."

Andy identified the inmate who was not wearing a mask as Obadiah Miller. Obadiah, nicknamed OB, was the primary aggressor. He was the one that was in front of Floyd punching him, and it appeared that he was also stabbing him. Andy stated that he had something in his hands.

The inmates were able to successfully handcuff Floyd behind his back. Now that the officer was subdued, they continued to beat and punch Floyd as they overpowered him. He was bleeding from his face, chest and ribs.

He was then dragged to the mop closet and thrown inside. He managed to call out "Code One" once more before he was locked in.

Chapter 4

Jordan Peters

That same morning, Jordan Peters, a Corrections Officer, worked a shift that went from 8 am to 4 pm. He had only worked at Vaughn for two years, and he did not have any experience working in the Department of Corrections before.

As part of his morning routine, he patrolled the perimeter by vehicle during the course of the day. At around 10:20 a.m., as he was passing by another police officer's radio, he heard the Code at Building C from their radio. Due to the fact that he did not have a radio with him, he dashed to Building C in an attempt to obtain one.

He was the first to arrive on the scene. He was soon joined by other officers. As he looked through the front door of the Sergeant's office, he observed blood splatters everywhere as he looked through the window.

It was around this time that Lt. Sennett arrived with a few other officers.

There was an open door at the top of the tier, but Peters did not see anyone. In the distance, he could see Mrs. May being bound and shackled in the office of the Counselor. As he walked towards the Counselor's office, his eyes grew wide.

Peters said that he couldn't tell if this was a test or if this was the real deal, and he wondered whether it was a test.

It was only after Peter heard the other officer, Lt. Sennett say,*"We 're out of here; they've taken over the building,"* that he accompanied the officers as they walked out of the C Building.

He recalls that while leaving there was a blood stain on the window of the chow room and nothing else on the floor except blood. As he walked out of the building, he noticed that all the windows in the B Tier were covered and that the inmates were sitting or lying in their cells.

Lieutenant Sennett

Lieutenant Sennett worked the 8am to 4pm shift as well. During the 13 years he had worked at the Delaware Department of Corrections, he was the Area Supervisor for the Delaware Department of Corrections. All of which were at Vaughn.

Among his duties, he dealt with issues, complaints, and incidents that involved inmates. He was in charge of a number of buildings, including building C.

The moment he heard 'Code One' (assault on an officer) a few minutes after ten in the morning, he immediately knew that this day would be different from the rest.

It was unclear who had initially made the call, but he was the only one who had access to the building, and he was the only one in the field. In the first couple of minutes after the code had been announced, Sennett, Corrections Officers Scott, Peter and Canon began to prepare for the entry into Building C.

After they opened the door, their eyes were drawn to the locker boxes and the pools of blood that were sprawled across the floor. A and B

Tier's doors were opened, and although no one was there, there appeared to be smoke coming from B Tier.

It was at that moment that Sennett said he heard Sgt. Floyd screaming from inside a closet. He recalls that he said, *"They took over the building. It's a setup. Get Out!"*

Winslow Smith

Winslow Smith had been employed by the Department of Corrections since 2001. The only job he had done previously was that of a lifeguard. After voluntarily resigning from the Department of Corrections in 2004, he worked a variety of other jobs before returning to the Department of Corrections in 2008. In addition to being married, Smith has three children.

A group of at least five inmates attacked him during the day shift on the morning of the uprising. As he recalled, all of them were wearing masks and carrying weapons at the time.

A blunt object struck him in the head, and he was knocked to the ground after he was struck with the object. In spite of his being conscious throughout the attack, his sight was not blurred.
    He was also able to see Sgt. Floyd and Guard Joshua Wilkinson being assaulted by inmates. One of the attackers managed to grab one end of his handcuffs, and while he was holding back, he was able to seize his right arm and cuff it.

When he finally managed to make it to the office, he was dragged back, beaten, and his other hand was cuffed in front of him. Initially, they beat Smith and threatened to throw him into a cell, but in the end, they decided to confine him to a small maintenance closet.

He was now handcuffed behind his back and his keys as well as the equipment that he had been using had been confiscated. The closet was then locked behind him.

Joshua Wilkinson

One year before the uprising, Joshua Wilkinson joined the department. He recalls between ten and fifteen prisoners attacking him. According to Smith, all inmates wore masks, and he was beaten and tortured. While he was unable to see Sgt. Floyd or Officer Smith during the attack, he heard Floyd yelling "Code One".

They stripped his equipment, handcuffed him, and threw him in a closet. Smith was confined to the same closet soon after.

****

Chapter 5

The inmates also set a trap to capture the first responder Quick Response Team ("QRT") officers. Multiple fires were started by inmates, activating sprinkler systems. They then waited for the QRT to arrive, hiding further down near the closets where Sgt. Floyd, Officer Smith, and Officer Wilkinson had been imprisoned.

Four QRT officers responded to the alert and alarms, running into Building C. They saw blood on every surface and were approaching the closet where, unknowingly, Sgt. Floyd was held. When the QRT officers entered his closet, Sergeant Floyd heard them.

As he smelled the fire and heard the alarms and sprinklers activate, Sgt. Floyd was probably aware that the inmates were setting a trap to capture the QRT. As the QRT approached, Sgt. Floyd yelled, *"It's a trap!" It's a trap! Go back! Get out of the building! Cut off the water!"*

After hearing the warnings and instructions from Sgt. Floyd, the QRT officers reluctantly complied with the warnings and instructions, quickly evacuating Building C and locking the door in order to contain the uprising and prevent it from spreading to the other buildings at Vaughn.

As they sat in their closet, Officers Smith and Wilkinson could hear the sounds of the inmates brutally beating and sadistically torturing Sgt. Floyd. It was not possible for them to help him because he was hand-cuffed and imprisoned, so they were powerless to intervene and help him. The closet in which Officer Smith and Wilkinson were imprisoned was relatively small, but it was large enough for both of them to be seated on the floor without strain.

While officers Smith and Wilkinson were imprisoned in the closet, the inmates threatened to kill them if they looked at their faces, and they continued to torture them while they were being held captive.

One of the inmates also unlocked the door and threw a burning blanket onto Officer Wilkinson. Because of his hands being cuffed behind his back, Officer Wilkinson was not able to remove the burning blanket from his body.

However, because his hands were cuffed in front of him, Officer Smith was able to eventually douse the blanket with the water accumulating on the floor from the sprinklers.

Smith and Wilkinson sat in the dark, huddled together, in the closet, they both suffered from severe injuries and were bleeding profusely. Officer Wilkinson's face was fully covered in blood, and he was bleeding profusely.

As they were inside the closet, they could hear the inmates moving footlockers in the area and were convinced that the inmates were barricading the door of the building because they believed that the inmates were barricading the exit.

The inmates eventually took Officer Smith and made him memorize five names. He was told by his captors that he was going to be released with the task to deliver these five names to the authorities outside of the prison.

There was a request by Smith that the inmates release Officer Wilkinson in his place, but this was refused by the inmates. The inmates made

Smith cover his head and place his back against the closet door. After unlocking the closet, they moved him out of it, and then locked the door again after they had moved him out of it.

They told him that they would kill him if he turned around or looked at them. A few minutes later, the inmates released him into the yard, where he was later rescued by the guards. The release took place at approximately 2:25 p.m. After Officer Smith was released, Officer Wilkinson lost consciousness numerous times due to his injuries and blood loss.

It was several hours after Smith's release that the inmates took Wilkinson out of the closet and showed him to the hostage negotiators through a window, demonstrating their willingness to release him.

As time went by, one of the inmates told Wilkinson that his being beaten, tortured, and held as a hostage was nothing personal, but that things would change at the Department of Corrections in terms of how they were treated as inmates.

By this time, Wilkinson was already concerned for Sgt. Floyd, and asked if he could talk to Sgt. Floyd, to which he was told that he could not do. In light of this, Wilkinson adduced the conclusion that Sgt. Floyd would not survive the attack.

While still handcuffed in the closet, one of the inmates entered the closet with a handheld radio and a homemade knife, holding the large blade up to Wilkinson's throat and making a threat to kill him with the weapon.

During the course of this exchange, the inmate ordering Wilkinson to listen to the radio message was shouting that the inmate was threatening to kill him, and Wilkinson complied with his orders.

Wilkinson was eventually retrieved from the closet by the inmates who had covered his head with a pillowcase and made him walk into the yard where he was rescued from the closet. It was sometime around the time of 8:00 p.m.

Chapter 6

Hammond, McCall, and Tuxward

After retreating to the basement, Officers Hammond, McCall, and Tuxward, immediately designated Officer Hammond to call in the recent events.

A *"Code One"* was immediately transmitted to Hammond's radio, indicating that an attack on staff was underway, as well as a *"Code Three"* that indicated a major disturbance was underway.

The codes were first called into the maintenance channel, but Officer Hammond was unable to receive any response to his call, so he called them into the general channel.

In addition, he also reported that Sgt. Floyd had been seriously injured, imprisoned by the inmates in the closet, and that the inmates had taken control of the entire unit.

In the first hour following the uprising, the rescue effort was fully informed that Sgt. Floyd's life was in jeopardy and that he needed to be rescued as soon as possible before his life was lost.

As much as Hammond, McCall, and Tuxward did not want to be in the basement, they still found themselves trapped there. They had no way out. It was clear to them that the only thing standing between them and severe physical injury or death was the single lock at the top of the stairs that sealed the door.

There was already no doubt that the inmates already had access to keys since they had been able to secure Sgt. Floyd inside the closet by quickly locking him in.

In addition, McCall stood lookout on top of the stairwell and relayed whatever information he was able to observe or hear to Hammond who relayed it to Tuxward.

Finally, McCall would relay the information to the prison authorities, either by telephone or radio, in both cases. It was while McCall was positioned at the lookout position that he witnessed an inmate approaching the door wearing a mask and armed with a large blade. In addition, he observed that both masked and unmasked inmates were carrying a radio, knives, and a large set of keys in their possession.

Their assumption was that they were trying to find just the right set of keys to open the basement door in order to attack them as soon as they found the key.

After a while, the inmates blocked the view from the basement door, so they would no longer be able to see what was happening in the unit or report what was happening there.

It was then that the smell of smoke began to fill their nostrils.

Soon after, they heard that the fire alarms and sprinkler system had gone off. As a result of the sprinklers, water flowed down the walls, into the basement, covering the floor and running down the walls as well.

Above them, they were hearing a lot of movement, with items being moved, dropped, and broken. They all felt uneasy, as their ears were ringing.

When the sprinklers went off, the phones switched off, leaving the only form of communication radio, which was their only means of reaching the outside world.

There was a growing sense of panic as the men wanted to escape the basement, but they were unable to do so due to the severe state of their situation. It was while they were in the basement at the prison where Hammond, McCall, and Tuxward heard the inmates make threats to kill all of the correctional officers who they had taken hostage.

In the basement, there was no way to lock the door to the boiler room. As they expected the armed inmates to attack them at any minute, they barricaded the boiler room door with, among other things, a picnic table and a concrete barrier, and stocked themselves with pipes, fire extinguishers, and other items to defend themselves from the inmates.

The Officers had repeatedly switched off the gas, electrical power, hot water supply, and water supply to the building on a number of occasions during their basement imprisonment.

Additionally, they reset the phones, and then turned the water back on again, all as instructed by the prison authorities who assisted them during the process.

As the men listened to the outside negotiators on the radio, the inmates verbally communicated their demands to the outside negotiators. Among them was the demand to speak with Governor Carney, but this request was denied.

It was between twelve to thirteen hours of being imprisoned in the basement of the prison, the prison authorities found a way to bring them to safety. It was instructed to them that they should access the attic slowly, carefully, and quietly, climb a cupola-like structure, make their way to the roof, and then walk very quietly and cautiously on the roof above the rioting prisoners.

In the end, Officers Hammond, McCall, and Tuxward were able to escape from the roof.

Chapter 7

In accordance with historical practices, CERT is prepared to regain control of the building and is capable of doing so.

According to the reports, on September 2, 1971, a riot took place in Building C, which led to the capture of three correctional officers. When the building was recaptured after three hours, they were rescued without any serious harm after they had been trapped for three hours.

The CERT's intended rescue actions were in compliance with the DCC's written standard operating procedures for the seizure and taking of hostages at a building in accordance with the Standard Operating Procedures.

The Warden, David Pierce, had given the go-ahead for the retaking of the building and the rescue of Sgt. Floyd and all the other hostages before their lives were further endangered. Rather than the Warden overseeing the rescue attempt, Governor Carney intervened, overruled him, and halted the rescue attempt for reasons that are unclear.

Upon hearing that Governor Carney had intervened in the situation, Warden Pierce was furious as he felt that his intervention had placed the lives of Sgt. Floyd and the other hostages at greater risk. As a result, the Governor decided that a rescue attempt would be attempted the next day.

On February 2, 2017, just before 5:06 a.m., in the early hours of February 2, 2017, the Governor's belated rescue effort was launched.

In the early hours of Saturday morning, SWAT teams from the Delaware State Police and the Maryland State Police stormed Building C and put an end to the uprising.

Lt. Brian Vanes, a DOC facility investigator and CERT team member, which breached the building during the response in the early morning hours of Feb. 2. He first found Floyd in the mop closet.

"I opened the door--" he said, choking up. After a long pause he continued, *"kind of hoping that Sgt. Floyd was going to be in [there] alive...I quick looked in I didn't see anything first, [then] I looked straight down and that's when I saw him...on the floor."*

Floyd's body was discovered under a pile of mattresses. Cpl. Timothy Aube, a paramedic with the Delaware State Police, encountered Floyd around 5:30 a.m. on Feb. 2, 2017.

"Floyd was face down; he had a lot of debris covered on top of him, I think there was mattresses, I remember the floor was like--I don't know, they had done something to flood the area. There was a lot of water on the floor, about an inch of water, and there was a lot of debris, trash, newspapers, and everything," he said.

He said Floyd was unresponsive, and his body was cold to the touch, signifying he'd been dead for quite some time. Aube described Floyd's injuries.

"I remember originally looking at his head, and it appeared that he had been struck with some kind of heavy object--I don't know what it was, but there was a pretty large balloon on the left side of his head, and then I remember on his back...it appears that he had sustained some kind of burning injury—I don't know if that was after he died or when he had sustained the injury--but there was no active bleeding obviously because he had no pulse, and there was also blood, kind of surrounding him in a couple areas, sort of on the floor next to him."

It is believed to have been murdered at some point after Officer Hammond informed the prison management of Sgt. Floyd's desperate condition. It is believed that the inmates moved and then murdered at some point after that.

Chapter 8

It wasn't long before the news of the riot began to spread and people began to arrive at the prison. The News Journal, Delaware's largest newspaper, had been requested by the prisoners early in the uprising.

Messages and phone calls had been funneled by family and friends of the prisoners to the News Journal. They made it clear that they were not rioting in order to cause unnecessary violence and destruction, but to protest this injustice.

They knew that would be the way the prison officials were going to portray it, so they prepared for it accordingly. The reasons and motivations for the riot were revealed early on.

Over the years, allegations of abuse by staff, inhumane conditions, and inconsistent policies were well-known grievances to both those working inside of the prison and the loved ones of those outside of the prison.

Those beliefs were echoed in a phone call between an inmate and his fiancée just minutes before the riot began.

Excerpts played at one of the trials included the inmate, Anthony Morrow saying, *"These cops be oppressing people."* and went into detail: *"these cops be spraying people, beating people, disrespecting them, talking about their families…"*

"This is the shit that goes on, babe- you don't know what goes on in here." "Yeah, he's stabbed up, you're fucking right he's hurt. He might have been talking to the wrong motherfucker… he's fucking him up! Yeah, they fuckin' Floyd up."

Protestors, as well as family and friends of the prisoners, arrived at the prison to show support. There are rarely happy endings in these situations.Inmate safety and well-being were deeply concerned amidst the fears expressed by family, friends, and even the public. There was every reason to worry.

During the hostage situation, emotions were running high, with at least four prison staff members being held as hostages by the inmates. It is likely that, once the police regained control of the building, the innocent, as well as the guilty, would either be hurt or killed when they regained control.

It would be unlikely that the police would take the time to investigate the involvement of any of the prisoners once they gained entry inside.

There was constant contact between the inmates and the News Journal during this time. The inmates talked of the abuse and mistreatment of the prisoners which led to the uprising and riot.

"We're trying to explain the reasons for doing what we're doing. Donald Trump. Everything that he did. All the things that he's doing now. We know that the institution is going to change for the worse.

We know the institution is going to change for the worse. We got demands that you need to pay attention to, that you need to listen to and you need to let them know.

Education, we want education first and foremost. We want a rehabilitation program that works for everybody. We want the money to be allocated so we can know exactly what is going on in the prison, the budget."

The inmate in charge (later identified as Royal Downs) went on to state that the uprising on February, 1st, 2017, came after several peaceful protests. He stated that this was a breaking point.

Most recently, two weeks before the riot, Royal Downs headed the protest where inmates refused to return to their cells after recreation time until they were allowed to speak with a supervisor about housing conditions.

The requests were ignored. Instead, some correctional officers, including Floyd, told superiors that the instigators of that Jan. 15 incident should be moved to another building for security reasons.

In the days and weeks that followed the standoff at the prison, the friends and families of the inmates at Vaughn became increasingly concerned.

There was no communication between any of the inmates and their families. Several weeks would go by without a word, followed by 'letters' sent on scraps of paper and on the back of medical request forms asking for help.

The letters detailed how several inmates were severely beaten and tortured in the days that followed the uprising and denied medical attention. The families sought answers and news media followed closely for any developments.

Chapter 9

In the aftermath of the riot, there was a mix of reactions. In spite of the tragic events that occurred at the prison on that fateful day at Vaughn, particularly the murder of Sgt Floyd, there was unexpected support for the inmates during that time.

In protest, people expressed their thoughts on social media, in the news, and in protests alike; following the prison riot, what reasons led the prisoners to stage a riot and takeover.

In the days and weeks following the siege, the events of that day became more clear as more details became available about it.

Although Building C was a Medium to Maximum Security housing unit, it was not equipped with cameras. Additionally, it appears that during the course of law enforcement regaining control of the unit, the entire building was virtually destroyed during the process of returning control to the authorities.

There would then be a task for investigators to try to piece together what happened on that day by trying to gather the evidence.

In the aftermath of a lengthy string of nonviolent protests by prisoners, it is assumed that the uprising took place because their grievances had not been resolved by the prison management.

As far as is known, several inmates were involved in the takeover of the prison; two officers were badly injured and one officer was killed in the incident.

As soon as the Detectives and Investigators arrived, they began talking to the prisoners, most of whom had been in the hospital for injuries they sustained as a result of being beaten by the police when they regained control and entered the building.

It would be fair to assume that most of the inmates were not thrilled to talk to the police after being severely beaten in a riot that the majority were not involved in.

A number of prisoners claim that they were tortured, beaten and deprived of any medical treatment in the days and weeks following the uprising because of the brutality of the guards.

It is evident from the medical records and letters sent to loved ones that the assertion has merit. Several inmates also reported that they were forced to listen to a call in news radio station where callers called for the execution of all the inmates.

Generally speaking, inmates have a tendency to stand together in solidarity with one another, which is well known. There was a connection between them all irrespective of whether they were innocent or guilty.

In the eyes of the law, most prisoners are guilty until the law proves that they are innocent. For the murder of Sgt. Floyd, it would be fair to say that the police would not only be seeking a conviction, but they would also be seeking revenge and retribution.

In the absence of cameras located within the prison, it would be necessary for someone to be able to tell what had happened. In order for them to be able to do this, someone had to be willing to step outside of the solidarity that the inmates shared between them.

As it turned out, the task turned out to be quite simple, as on October 17, 2017, there were indictments handed down against 18 inmates; 16 of the 18 were being charged with Floyd's murder.

The 16 inmates faced three murder counts each in Floyd's death (intentional murder, felony murder, and recklessly causing the death of a correctional officer), as well as assault, kidnapping, riot, and conspiracy charges were Jarreau Ayers, Abednego Baynes, Kevin Berry, John

Bramble, Abdul-Haqq El-Qadeer, aka Louis Sierra, Deric Forney, 28; Kelly Gibbs, Robert Hernandez, Janiis Mathis, Lawrence Michaels, Obadiah Miller, Jonatan Rodriguez, Alejandro Rodriguez-Ortiz, Roman Shankaras, Corey Smith, and Dwayne Staats.

Two others faced kidnapping, riot, and conspiracy counts: Pedro Chairez, 42; and Royal Downs, 52.

There was a decision made that the inmates would be tried in groups rather than individually.

On October 21, 2018, it was reported that one of the prisoners who was indicted following the riot, but not charged with murder, had pleaded guilty to the charges against him before the first trial was to be held. In this case, he would be acting as a witness against the other prisoners in the case. The prisoner, Royal Downs, was held in an undisclosed location, separate from his co-defendants, and his court records were sealed at the time of his arrest.

As a result, The Vaughn 18 became the Vaughn 17.

Aria Orchard

Chapter 10

Jarreau Ayers was serving a life sentence for the January 2000 murder of Wilmington, Delaware Resident, Arthur Wells. While incarcerated, he was also charged with the murder of another Wilmington Resident, David Butler from 1997. Ayers made the decision to represent himself less than a month before jury selection began in this trial due to a last-minute conflict discovered between his court-appointed defense attorney and a potential witness.

Dwayne Staats was serving also serving a life sentence for the April 2004 murder of a 31-year-old Wilmington Resident. Like Ayers's, he also chose to represent himself for the trial.

Deric Forney was serving an 11-year sentence for possession of a firearm during the commission of a felony. He was also charged and convicted in 2013 for Violation of probation when he was found to have in is possession a gun and drugs.

Forney chose to be represented by Attorney Ben Gifford.

Abednego Baynes had been in and out of the court system dating back to the age of 16. He was serving an 18-year sentence for second degree murder.

Kevin Berry was serving a 14-year sentence for 3 counts of First Degree Robbery. At the time of the uprising, he had roughly two years left to complete his sentence.

John Bramble was serving a 40-year sentence for Possession of a Firearm During the Commission of a Felony, Assault Second Degree, Possession of a Firearm by a Person Prohibited, Possession of Ammunition by a Person Prohibited, and Home invasion.

Abdul-Haqq El-Qadeer AKA Luis Sierra, wa serving a life sentence for First degree murder.

Kelly Gibbs was serving a 24-year sentence for Second Degree Murder.

Robert Hernandez,was transferred to Vaughn from New Mexico and was serving a 16-year sentence for Second degree murder.

Janiis Mathis was serving a 15-year sentence for Second Degree assault.

Lawrence Michaels was serving 19 years for Kidnapping in the 1st Degree, Attempted Robbery in the 1st Degree, and Possession of a Firearm during Commission of a Felony.

Obadiah Miller was serving 10 years for Manslaughter and Possession of a Firearm During the Commission of a Felony.

Jonatan Rodriguez serving 40 years for Manslaughter. He was convicted of murdering the two-year-old daughter of his girlfriend.

Roman Shankaras was serving a 7-year sentence for robbery and a riot. Initially, it was believed that he was the mastermind behind the riot because of his previous conviction.

Corey Smith was serving 14 year sentence for second-degree assault, promoting prison contraband, among other charges.

Alejandro Rodriguez-Ortiz was serving 40 years for manslaughter.

Pedro Chairez was transferred from Arizona serving a 43-year sentence for Murder 2nd and other charges committed in that state.

Royal Downs was transferred from Maryland serving a life sentence for Murder 1st Degree, Conspiracy and other charges committed in that state.

Chapter 11

Sgt. Steven R. Floyd, Sr. was born in Lewes, Delaware in 1969. He was raised in Millsboro and attended Sussex Central High School.

After graduation, he entered the U.S. Army, quickly rose to the rank of Sergeant First Class. He served as an Armor Tank Crewman in the Tank Corps, and was a veteran of Operation Desert Storm.

He joined the defendant Department of Correction, State of Delaware ("DOC") in May 2000, and was a Correctional Officer. He spent his entire career at Vaughn Correctional Center where he eventually was promoted to Sergeant.

In 2016, he received the Warden's Award for his outstanding performance working with staff members and the public. Following the tragic events at the center of this case, he was posthumously awarded the Medal of Valor and promoted to Lieutenant.

Lt. Floyd was involved in the community providing donations for back-to-school and two sports programs, organizing community unity events, and many programs that supported the homeless and veterans.

He supported diabetes, breast cancer and other life-threatening disease awareness through education and fund-raising. He married

Saundra M. Floyd in 1988. They had three children, Candyss C. White, Steven R. Floyd, Jr., and Chyvante E. Floyd. At the time of his death, Candyss, the oldest daughter was 31 years old, married and has one child. Steven R. Floyd, Jr., Lt. Floyd's namesake and middle child, lived in Virginia. He was 29 years old and has one child.

Chyvante E. Floyd, the youngest daughter of Sgt. Floyd, who lived in Delaware, was 20 years old and was enrolled as a student at Delaware State University majoring in Sociology.

Sgt. Floyd was laid to rest on February 11, 2017. The first public viewing was held on Friday, Feb. 10, 2017, at Delaware State University Memorial Hall. He was given a hero's homecoming. Hundreds of mourners and law enforcement officials came to show their support and respect for the fallen officer.

Chapter 12

A lawsuit was filed on April 18, 2017, on behalf of the family of Sgt. Floyd and the DOC staff who were victims of the uprising.

Plaintiffs in the lawsuit include Saundra Floyd and her family, Officers Winslow Smith, Joshua Wilkinson, Justin Tuxward, Matthew McCall, and Owen Hammond.

There were six defendants; Jack Markell, Ruth Ann Minner, Stanley W. Taylor, Jr., The Honorable Carl C. Danburg, Robert Coupe, Ann Visalli, Brian Maxwell, Perry Phelps, Michael S. Jackson, and the Department of Correction, State of Delaware.

According to the lawsuit, each of the individual defendants was responsible for the uprising, injuries sustained in the uprising, and Sgt. Floyd's death.

The lawsuit stated, in part, that;

"This is a civil action for compensatory and punitive damages brought by the Estate and survivors of a deceased Correctional Officer as well as five fellow Correctional Officers who survived torture, death threats and beatings in the inmate uprising (the "Uprising") in the Delaware prison system on February 1 and 2, 2017, which was proximately caused by the actions and policies of the individual defendants, in violation of the plaintiffs' rights to substantive due 1 process under the Fourteenth Amendment of the U.S. Constitution."

It further went on to state;

1. The Contractual Obligation to Provide "Sufficient Staffing" for a "Safe and Secure" work environment.

2. Severe understaffing was hidden from the public and the Legislature.

3. Numerous staffing and security problems were caused by these cuts and the exodus of correctional officers.

4.DOC instituted a policy of "freezing" or forced involuntary overtime whereby correctional officers were forced to stay on at the end of their shifts, and to work another shift, because there was no other officer to replace them.

5. In May 2004, the DOC was over an entire shift short which resulted in a mass amount of involuntary overtime or freezing of officers.

6. Several buildings at DCC were closed because of the lack of staff.

7.Any correctional officer who refused to be "frozen" and work the forced, involuntary, mandatory overtime, was charged with abandonment of post or other disciplinary measures which resulted either in suspension or termination of employment.

8. Due to understaffing, Defendants adopted numerous dangerous policies. For example, the DOC had a policy of not searching inmates, including violent ones, who were being transported to court for hearings.

9. Other dangerous and harmful policies, practices or customs enacted by the Minner(Gov. Ruth Ann Minner) defendants in this time period included: not searching prisoners resident within the prisons for contraband, such as weapons, and propping open locked security doors

with pieces of wood, so that they no longer functioned as security doors.

10. Essential Officer Training also was eliminated. For example, no training was ever given to correctional officers by DOC on how to transport inmates to or from prison.

11. This lack of training in various areas led to numerous high profile major security breakdowns, including: December 2003 - a convicted felon escaped from DOC custody while en route to court, triggering a massive three-week manhunt.

12. April 2004 , a defendant during a rape trial slit his own neck in open court with a razor blade during the trial.

13. April 2004, a prisoner at Vaughn was attacked and severely injured by another inmate with a razor.

14. April 2004, a convicted felon swallowed a handcuff key while on his way to a court hearing.

15. May 2004, that same felon again swallowed another handcuff key, this time while on his way to the hospital.

16. There were numerous additional incidents which were never publicly revealed.

In the spring of 2004 an outside DOC security expert and consultant publicly released a report harshly criticizing the DOC and squarely placing responsibility upon the Minner defendants and the DOC administration for numerous security lapses.

The expert concluded that "somebody is going to be seriously injured or killed" unless things change. This same DOC outside expert harshly criticized the Minner defendants and the DOC administration for their lackadaisical approach to prison safety.

In the spring and summer of 2004 there was a flood of newspaper articles and media attention about the many dire safety issues plaguing the DOC, including severe understaffing, major security lapses caused by the understaffing, the lack of training, and other problems.

Because of this media attention, through internal reports and by other means, the Minner defendants had actual knowledge of all of the many dangerous understaffing and safety issues plaguing the DOC.

The regular response of the defendants to security incidents in 2004 was that "inmates do stupid things."

Tragically, one of the incidents included in the suit was the rape and attempted murder of a female counselor.

On July 12, 2004, An inmate serving 660 years for rape, who was armed with an 8-inch shank and other contraband equipment, attacked, immobilized and took a female civilian counselor hostage for 6 ½ hours.

During this time he repeatedly raped her, all before he was eventually shot and killed by a correctional officer on the Correctional Emergency Response Team ("CERT") crawling through the ceiling as the inmate fought to murder this innocent women with his shank.

The root cause of this incident was understaffing in the DCC which caused numerous security breakdowns that day.

These breakdowns included: security doors being left open instead of being locked and secured; security doors being propped open with pieces of wood instead of being locked and secured; a single untrained correctional officer being required to monitor electronic displays for an entire section of the building, a job intended for three correctional officers, not one; insufficient numbers of "rovers" being assigned to the building; lack of searches for weapons and other contraband; and other breakdowns.

The Minner defendants repeatedly and publicly lied and denied that the severe levels of dangerous understaffing had played any role whatsoever in the security breakdowns leading to the abduction, rape, and attempted murder of this innocent woman.

Defendant Minner's official public response to this unprecedented security breakdown was "In prisons, you almost expect this to happen."

In the end, the Plaintiffs were all awarded an undisclosed settlement.

Chapter 13

Monday, October 22, 2018, marked the beginning of the trial for the first group of defendants. On trial, there were three prisoners who were being held.

The first, Jarreau Ayers, who was currently serving a life sentence for first-degree murder, the second was Deric Forney, who was serving 11 years on conviction of possession of a firearm in the course of committing a felony, and the third, Dwayne Staats, who was serving a life sentence for murder.

As the presiding judge in the case, William C Carpenter, Jr. would preside over the proceeding.

Judge Carpenter was appointed in 1993 to the New Castle County Delaware Superior Court, reappointed in 2005, and reappointed for a third term in 2017.

Carpenter worked as a private practice attorney prior to his position with the New Castle County Courts. Carpenter worked briefly as an attorney for a private practice after graduating from law school. He then became Assistant United States Attorney for over 8 years.

In 1985, President Reagan appointed him to be the District of Delaware's United States Attorney. He continued in this position through the Bush and Clinton administrations.

The case would be prosecuted by Deputy Attorney General John Downs. He was formerly the pastor of Grace Baptist Church where he served for nearly five years, prior to being appointed to AG Downs' position.

His professional experience spans nearly 30 years. From 1982 until 2003, he worked as a police officer in New Castle County, and since 2003, he has worked as an attorney for the State of Delaware-assigned to the homicide unit.

He was joined by Brian Robertson, an Attorney with the firm, and Nichole Warner, an Attorney with the firm, as co-counsels.

Both Dwayne Staats and Jarreau Ayers made the decision to act as their own lawyers, which is something that many lawyers would strongly advise against.

Staats had admitted to being the mastermind behind the uprising, but he maintains that he did not kill anyone during the riot. Before this admission was made, another inmate, Roman Shankaras, had been accused of being the mastermind in the case prior to this admission.

Staats was convicted of First Degree murder when he was twenty-three years old. He received a life sentence for the murder of a 31-year-old man in Wilmington, Delaware.

He already intended to represent himself for several months after he was indicted. State prosecutors have said he commandeered one of the walkie-talkies used in hostage negotiations and some inmates have said he helped carry out the riot.

Staats argued that he didn't wear a mask on Feb. 1, 2017, and that the jury must see the "collage of misinformation" the state presents for what it really is.

Jarreau Ayers was convicted of First Degree Murder in April of 2011 and sentenced to serve a life sentence. While incarcerated, he confessed to the cold case 1997 murder of David Butler, a Wilmington Resident.

He was given an additional life sentence for the murder. Unlike Staats, Ayers made the decision to represent himself less than a month before jury selection began in this trial due to a last-minute conflict discovered between his court-appointed defense attorney and a potential witness.

Deric Forney was a serving an eleven-year sentence for possession of a firearm in the commission of a felony. He was the only one of the first group to be represented by an Attorney.

Ben Gifford was court appointed to represent Forney.

"We are not starting out on a level playing field," Gifford told the jury during opening statements. *"You can't vote guilty until the state gets you there. It's the state's burden to overcome the presumption of innocence."*

Several revelations were made during the trial, and one concerned the role of Royal Downs, the only inmate who had voluntarily spoken with investigators and agreed to testify for the State in exchange for a plea deal with the State.

Chapter 14

Royal Diamond Downs was born on August 13, 1968, in Baltimore Maryland. In terms of his criminal record, he has a long list of offenses dating back to 1990. The most serious offense occurred in 1994. On June 13, 1994.

Downs was arrested and subsequently found guilty of both murder and conspiracy in Baltimore, Maryland. His sentence included not only the imposition of life without parole, but he was also sentenced to serve an additional 20 years on the basis of his involvement in the conspiracy.

Interestingly enough, Downs was charged in Baltimore with causing a riot at the prison he was serving time in. He was charged for his role in causing it.

Immediately after being charged, Downs contacted the States Attorney's Office to arrange a meeting in order to discuss crimes committed by his former associates in order to obtain a lighter sentence for his crimes.

There is no question that Downs was a leader of The Black Guerrilla Gang in prison, and his testimony against other members would put his life in danger if he remained in a Maryland prison for the duration of his sentence.

The testimony he provided against his co-defendant, Boris Bell, resulted in him being re-sentenced on November 8, 1996, to a total of 10 years in prison for the conspiracy charge. He also qualified for parole for the charge of First Degree Murder.

As of the date of the publication of this book, he had two parole hearings. As a result of his testimony in Maryland, he was transferred to Vaughn Prison.

After the riot, Downs gave statements to the police on four separate occasions. The first of these was on February 2, 2017, which was the day after the riot had taken place.

Although it is unknown whether detectives were aware of his involvement in a riot at his former prison, or the fact that he was turning state evidence against his former gang in order to reduce his sentence and be transferred to another prison, it is possible that they were aware of both of those things.

Royal Downs spoke with detectives several times over the course of the investigation. On one of those occasions, he approached detectives and asked for a deal, letting them know that he had previously worked with the police in Maryland to convict former members of gangs in exchange for a lighter sentence.

Staats was able to interview Downs at his trial, and Downs reduced the significance of his role in the uprising to a very small degree. When he was played back a recording of his conversation with the hostage negotiator, he absurdly claimed that it was not his voice, but Staats that was speaking. Even the Prosecutor, AG John Downs, who was appointed to prosecute the case, concluded that it was the voice of Royal Downs speaking.

The following is the account of the events on February 1, 2017, according to Royal Downs:

It was Downs assertion that he was only interested in peaceful protest activities and that he was only engaged in those. In his account of the morning of the uprising, Downs described walking around the yard with an inmate named Boston who he had met the previous day in the yard.

Before yard was called, Rome, (Roman Shankaras)Staats, Smoke (Lawrence Michaels), Capo(Jonatan Rodriguez), and Cream(Corey Smith), were having a conversation that he overheard. They were discussing events that were about to take place and going to take over C building. He claimed that he did not hear how, nor any exact details.

He saw that the named inmates had masks that they checked to make sure were good to use. When Floyd called the yard, half of the inmates complied.

He stated that he saw the men put on masks when they entered the building. Shortly after he heard Sgt. Floyd scream *"Code One."*

According to Downs, he kept walking around with Boston and fifteen to twenty minutes later, Smoke came to the door and called everyone to come in.

Everybody walked in, and Downs returned to his cell on C Tier. He stated that inmates came into his cell to tell him what had happened.

Downs' cellmate Kelly Gibbs came into the cell with blood on his clothes and Gibbs told him it was from Floyd. Gibbs then left to change clothes and had no weapons at that point. Downs left his cell and talked to people on C tier and someone said to push the locker boxes onto the tier, to which he complied.

Thirty to forty minutes later, Downs went to *"check on some associates of mine."*

He went to all the tiers and talked to a few people. He then states that he walked into the classroom and said that Dwayne Staats was negotiating on the radio.

He had a shank in his hand. Downs sat with Staats for a while listening, and left shortly after.

When he returned to the classroom the electricity, water, and phones had been turned off. He knew they wanted these things on. He knew they wanted the media for protection, electricity to see outside, and water for the bathrooms.

Downs said they needed protection because the administration at Vaughn was "murderous" and that if they came in they would do a lot of damage to people. Downs began negotiating for the above-listed things, because "nobody else stepped up."

He was aware of Smith, Wilkinson, Floyd, and May as hostages at this point. He claims to have talked to Mrs. May a few times (a claim she denies). He says he did not know what negotiations took place before he got involved.

During the first trial, the Prosecutor played state's Exhibit 289 for court.

"Man, Floyd already down. He bout to be cancelled."

Downs identified this voice as Dwayne Staats. Royal Downs stated that Staats was not around much when he was negotiating on the radio. He also stated that he was not involved with Smith's release.

He did however see Smith get released from someone else's cell window. He sat in the classroom negotiating, and walked around tiers and maintains that he was not involved. It was *"chaos"*, *"do as you please"*, and *"no order at all."*

Downs asserted that he was involved in Wilkinson's release and negotiated for a handcuff key.

Wilkinson's handcuffs were too tight, and his hands were swollen. He expressed that he was concerned for the officer.

He says that he spoke with hostage negotiator White, but Smith was the first person. In negotiations, Downs used the name Sam Cooke, and a few others when speaking to negotiators. Sam Cooke was chosen because of the song *"A Change Gonna Come."*

(The Prosecutor then played state's Exhibit 292.)

Negotiations about the cuff key, and how the inmates have been given nothing for three hours. Downs identified the voices as Dwayne Staats and Smoke on the clip.

Clip: *"You know why all this bullshit started?"* (different voices are talking) *"severe oppression"*, *"dehumanizing conditions"*, *"everything stays in house in here"*, *"no education curriculum"*, *"been going on for years."*

Downs states that Staats said some of these things, but that part *"might have been me"*, and *"I believe the first part was me."*

Next clip:

"This coulda been over", *"Where is Carney at?*(referring to Governor Carney)"* Downs identified this voice once again as Staats.

More clips are played and Downs identifies them all as Staats.

There were talks about the "prison pipeline" and at one point saying *"we're liberated."*

Downs stated he did not have any weapons or assault any Corrections Officers during the uprising. Although, he stated he saw two attacks, both on Floyd.

The first attack was in the mop closet. Inmates tried to choke and cut Floyd's throat. When asked who? Downs replied, *"J Rodriguez, Obadiah, and a couple more, but it was hard to see because the light was out in the closet."*

The second attack was outside the Sergeant's Office. And a few people were involved. Downs saw Floyd being dragged from the closet to the office. A fire extinguished was used as a weapon.

At this point, Downs admitted he has given three or four statements to the police and couldn't remember everything.

When asked, *"Why did you talk to the authorities?"* Downs said there were a couple of reasons.

Regardless of whether or not he talked on the radio, Downs says he believed he would have been one of the charged. He also had the opportunity to have an old conviction overturned.

The Prosecutor, clearly frustrated at the different narrative that Downs was providing in court, said he was going to read a statement Downs made wherein he said who he saw assault Floyd outside the Sgt's office. He stated that he wanted to "refresh his recollection."

He was clearly not happy that Downs did not name anyone in his testimony and wanted him to be forced to testify as to what he had told police when he made his plea deal.

Judge Carpenter stated that he would permit it, and that he would need to go a few steps further for impeachment.

It was then that Royal Downs made the following statements:

He was on B tier before Floyd was dragged from the closet. Luis Sierra came onto B tier and said that no one should come off the tier. Downs states that he left the tier and was not stopped by anyone. He then stated that it was Obadiah, Cut(Pedro Chairez), and one more that dragged Floyd.

He adds that Smoke was there, *"delegating"*. Cut sat on Floyd's back, and it looked like he had a razor. Cut was handed a fire extinguisher which he used to beat Floyd.

Downs says that he left and that was the last time he knows something happened to Floyd, and it was "an hour or two before I left the building."

The Prosecution stated once again that he wanted to "refresh his memory"to Downs by showing him his statement that he gave prior.

Downs says this is incorrect, that he was in the last group to leave. Wilkinson left the building, which was the wave before Downs.

He was then shown the photo book of all the inmates when he was interviewed by police.

The Prosecutor shows Downs pages from the book, and he begins to name the individuals that were named in the indictment.

The subject of prison kites came up and Downs communicated with inmate, Roman Shankaras via kites, and said *"I turnt em over to yall."*

(Kites refers to a written request for something.)

Downs had the kites given to someone else to hold in case he was charged, when he would tell the police to meet with the people holding the kites to receive them.

The kites were then shown to the defense. In cross-examination, Dwayne Staats, who was acting as his own attorney, quoted from a statement Downs made to Police on 2/2/17.

"I'm here from Baltimore. I absolutely have no problem assisting y'all."

Downs mentioned cooperating with Angela Smith, an FBI Agent in Baltimore. When asked if he had changed his life, he replied, *"Yes."*

Staats: *"You stepped away from BGF?"*

Downs: *"Yes."*

Staats: *"You didn't help U.S. Attorney General in Baltimore?"*

Downs: *" No."*

Staats: *"You gave no assistance?"*

Downs: *"Correct."*

Staats: *"That had nothing to do with why you were sent to Delaware?"*

Downs: *"No, it was because of my affiliation."*

An FBI agent familiar with Angela Smith asked Downs about his interactions with her during Downs' interview with police.

Downs: *"She chose not to use my testimony."*

FBI: *"But she still gave you what you needed?"*

Downs: *"Yeah, because she knew my life was in danger."*

It was also revealed that Downs has had the witness on his original murder conviction from Baltimore recant on her testimony. She contacted Downs, and he told the witness how to rewrite her affidavit to recant her testimony.

Staats: *"Do you know the general idea of a conspiracy?"*

Downs: *"Yes."*

Downs said there were two meetings before 2/1/2017 about having a protest in the yard.

At the meetings, Staats did not want to stand in the yard for a protest. During his 9/19 statement to police, Downs was shown the photo book.

When he saw Staats's face, he said, according the transcript: *"Actually I just, I didn't even know him in the building until after the situation happened."*

Staats:" *If you didn't know me in the building, why'd you put me in those conversations? Did the state tell you to do that?"*

Downs: *"No."*

Downs now states that he cannot recall if he negotiated for the release of Corrections Officer Smith or not. After coming into the building initially, Downs was on C tier for thirty to forty minutes before leaving.

Dwayne Staats referred to Downs as *"the most influential guy in Delaware history"*, and Downs denied this title.

Staats then played a clip of negotiations that had been previously played and identified as having Downs's voice by multiple witnesses. Downs did not recognize his own voice at least one time.

Staats: *"Was Floyd's murder the result of stalled or failed negotiations?"*

Downs: *"I don't know."*

When asked about using his influence to prevent inmates from killing rats and pedophiles during the uprising.

Downs: *"Well, it didn't happen, did it?"*

Downs was questioned about a recording of a phone call he made to his daughter on 1/20. The call was about Downs getting his daughter to get an ounce of weed for him. Downs admitted he wanted her to hold it for him.

Staats: *"How'd you plan on getting it into the prison?"*

Downs: *"There were a couple ways."*

Staats: *"You asked your daughter to risk her freedom for your satisfaction."*

Downs: *"I did."*

Staats: *"You still maintain you was saving lives?"*

Downs: *"Yes."*

Downs responded that he never said anything to Floyd, and never wanted Floyd to see his face.

When made a phone call to his family the night of 2/1/2017, his family told him they recognized his voice on the radio. Downs stayed off the radio and no longer negotiated.

Staats: *"So you just gave up your mission to save lives?"*

Downs *:* *" I know you wasn't there,"* referring to Staats.

Staats: *" Nobody asked why you was just standing there?"*

Downs: *"No."*

Staats: *"Seems like you personally had to make sure Floyd was dead before you left the building."*

Downs: *" No."*

Downs then asserts that he tried to get a kite to Sgt. Floyd before the uprising. His intent was to warn him that his life may be in danger.

This was the extent of Royal Downs's testimony. If you are to believe him, he maintains that he was not involved and stood around watching while everything was going on.

He further claims that not only was he trying to save lives, he actually tried to get a message to Sgt. Floyd that his life was in danger.

Chapter 15

On November 16, 2018,Attorney General John Downs began closing arguments for the State.

"February 1, 2017, there was a violent takeover of a building at James T. Vaughn Correctional Center. It was not a protest gone wrong- it was planned, organized attacks done simultaneously on staff. Correctional officers were restrained and shoved in closets. The terror began at 10:22am based on evidence.

According to Jarreau Ayers, inmates were liberated- they began to have fun, they were just walking around, cooking, talking, eating.

That is not what happened. It wasn't fun, it wasn't liberation. It was terror, there were injuries, there was restraint and there was death.

The investigation began that day. Sergeant Weaver and the Delaware State Police made sense of the scene.

There were 126 potential witnesses and 3 maintenance workers, and C.O.s Winslow Smith, Joshua Wilkinson and counselor Patricia May. There was a large, contaminated crime scene.

The investigation culminated October 2017 with the indictment of 18 people. 16 were charged with riot, murder, assault, kidnapping, and conspiracy. Royal Downs and Pedro Chairez were charged with riot and conspiracy.

For these 3 defendants- Jarreau Ayers, Dwayne Staats and Deric Forney there is evidence of larger conspiracy. There were assaults, we heard testimony about 'Smoke,' 'O.B.,' 'Capo,' 'Menace,' 'Cream' and 'Cut.' The evidence presented in this trial suggests that here are two of the leaders in the takeover of C Building and one soldier.

Dwayne Staats told you in a kite from the stand that this was his plan, his idea, his seed.

He started everything. He recruited lifers, people with nothing to lose. Jarreau Ayers was the shot caller, [according to evidence].

He was involved in planning and carrying the uprising out. Deric Forney was a soldier- he was involved in the attack on C.O. Wilkinson and restrained him so the bigger plan could be accomplished. The plan was to use weapons, force and violence- it was reasonably foreseeable that injuries and death could occur.

When people are charged with riot, two or more people engage in disorderly conduct with intent to commit felonies or misdemeanors.

It is a felony to assault a correctional officer. Riot is to create a public inconvenience by engaging in threatening, tumultuous behavior and can occur in any place not private. That includes prison.

When people are charged with murder in the first degree, under Delaware law, a person or persons who act can be charged with different counts for the same death, depending on what the state proves.

Intentional murder necessitates conscious objective and purpose. Reckless murder during a felony is to recklessly cause a death during commission of a felony.

The judge will explain that this is a difference in mindset- the state has to prove what's going on in the person's mind that they would disregard a risk that death would result from an action.

Murder in the first degree of a law enforcement officer in the performance of their duty is likewise reckless. This means to be aware of and consciously override knowledge that risk that death would result by their action.

Counts 5 and 6 are the assaults on C.O. Wilkinson and C.O. Smith. This can occur during riot and/or felony, involving injury, recklessly or not.

Counts 7, 8 and 9 are kidnappings- the judge will explain to you what is meant by 'unlawfully restrained.'

Kidnapping is to 'terrorize or inflict physical injury, to hold hostage and to not release the person unharmed in a safe place prior to trial.'

Count 11 is Conspiracy. This means that the person who committed conspiracy took a substantial step toward accomplishing what the evidence shows happened. The evidence suggests that that's exactly what happened.

The state has to prove beyond a reasonable doubt- this does not mean to overcome every possible doubt. It means that you are to assess the evidence, consider what you have heard and seen, and you need to be firmly convinced of defendants' guilt.

Use your common sense this is not a speculative, vague, amorphous idea. You need to hear, think about, talk about and question the evidence to reach a conclusion. The state endeavored to prove the defendants were involved in the riot, as accomplices they are responsible for acts that were committed.

We use the evidence to make this conclusion. To do this, we needed to prove a state of mind, a conscious object of purpose and an unjustifiable risk. We can infer what is going on in someone's mind by what they did. Evidence can be direct or circumstantial.

You saw the buildings during presentation of evidence, you have a good grasp on how C Building operated. You saw evidence of riot- 'tumultuous, threatening behavior.'

[AG Downs displays a picture of the inside of C Building that was part of evidence].

Building C was trashed it was flooded, there were fires set, things were strewn about the hallways, there were injuries to Correctional Officers.

This was tumultuous, threatening, disorderly conduct within a prison. Two were hurt and one was killed. The medical examiner said that Sergeant Floyd had multiple blunt force traumas.

He was beaten to death. He had blood loss because of injuries. He had wounds to his head and his back, and he died. There was not a fixed time of death of when this happened.

He died, sometime in that night- if he had been released; the injuries he sustained would not have caused his death. He was held until he was dead- the evidence is that when he was dead they took burning objects and threw them on him.

The burns on his face, back, and neck were postmortem. This is intentional murder. Sergeant Floyd was in the closet, we knew because Lieutenant Sennett testified about it, recounting when he was in the building.

We heard Code Three called. Sergeant Floyd is in the closet at that time, he tells Lieutenant Sennett 'it's a trap.'

Lieutenant Sennett testified that he wasn't going to justify the safety of who he had with him, or give them more hostages. Until the crew would secure the building, he backed out."

AG Downs continues.

"The hub area was blocked off- so you can't see out or in. The blankets and locker boxes were not there to block entry. They were there to block witnesses from seeing what people were doing in there, according to Corrections Officer's testimony.

Sitting in that darkened closet, people were throwing things on them; they could hear Sergeant Floyd screaming and being beaten.

Correctional Officer's. Smith and Wilkinson lived- Sergeant Floyd wasn't given that choice.

Witness Richard McCane testified that he heard Sergeant Floyd say, 'why are you doing this? I know who you are.'

Witness Henry Anderson testified that he heard Sergeant Floyd say 'I've seen your faces you're not going to get away with this.' Sergeant Floyd will never say that again.

He sees the assault, he sees Cut-and Jonatan Rodriguez -they hit him with a fire extinguisher, and covered him with mattresses.

AG Downs plays a recording from prior evidence of the prison police saying, *"Code Three", this is not a drill, inmates have seized the building."*

There's a sergeant in a utility closet. There was a riot. Sergeant Floyd ended up dead. He was killed during commission of a felony. The murder of a law enforcement officer in the commission of their duty- the judge will explain that a correctional officer is a law enforcement officer.

This was his career, it was a normal day. He called the tower, he got 'Code Green,' and he opened the door to the yard. That was the last normal thing he did- between when he called first yard, he was unaware that the plan had been put in place.

He was unaware that they had masks ready, gloves ready, weapons prepared. When they came in from first yard, Dwayne Staats said he sent the signal- he went to the counselor, he showed the knife. [As to quote Staats, AG Downs said]

"I put the knife in Ms. May's face, and it jumps off." There were 3 C.O.s to subdue. Sergeant Floyd was killed because he is a law enforcement officer. First degree kidnapping.

The C.O. witnesses were terrified. The Senior Officer, Winslow Smith, kept the Junior Officer, Joshua Wilkinson calm. In testimony, it was discussed that inmates came in to the office and asked for the computer password and the senior officer said just give it to them.

They were not released unharmed in a safe place prior to trial. They were released, but were harmed.

Patricia May was in the counselor's office on B Tier, then went to cell right 10 and then to right 4 or 5. The terror she had- an inmate with a knife, binding her hands, putting a hood over her head. Would she ever see her husband again?

She was not harmed physically, but was also not released in a safe place prior to trial. She was not released at all. They knew they lost the leverage they had.

In the negotiations, they did not say Sergeant Floyd was dead. They did mention Ms. May on the radio, and there were phone calls with Ms. May.

That is why the CERT team knew to go to B Tier- the decision was made to get the backhoe, to locate Patricia May. They knew she was there and alive- they didn't know about Sergeant Floyd. There was a breach, they went in, they retrieved Ms. May- jackpot. She was found alive.

Assault in the first degree: C.O.s Winslow Smith and Joshua Wilkinson. Winslow Smith had injuries to the neck, hands, a concussion, PTSD. He's had problems since then- anxiety, depression and nightmares because of injuries he sustained.

Joshua Wilkinson had facial fractures- his jaw, the orbital of his eye, the bone in his cheek was just, like, floating. He also had PTSD, a concussion, headache and migraines. These are serious physical injuries.

Accomplice liability means people were working together, and it establishes whether they can be held liable for the actions of another. A defendant can be convicted of an offense where the underlying offense is convicted by another. The distinction is aiding in the crime.

The 16 defendants did not all kill Sergeant Floyd. That is not in evidence. We don't know who inflicted the death blow; we don't have evidence that this person or that person did it.

We do know that they were working together to commit assault and riot- they are responsible for the actions of others as accomplices. Use your common sense.

If someone wants to go to the bank and needs a ride, then that someone robs the bank, and you're the driver- are you responsible? Delaware has a more nuanced understanding- if you didn't know the intent was to commit felony or misdemeanor offenses, you're merely present at the crime scene.

If you did know, it becomes a question of intent, whether you knew if it was reasonably foreseeable that a felony or misdemeanor would occur. The defendants have to have kind of the same mindset, to know what's happening. If they didn't plan to, but were involved with the action, was it reasonably foreseeable that someone could die because of the forcible takeover of C Building?

Because of this, one can be guilty as principal they did it- or guilty as an accomplice- they aided it. The crimes against Winslow Smith and Joshua Wilkinson were at B Tier and A Tier.

Against Sergeant Floyd was at the yard door. They had to be subdued simultaneously- there was no time to react, and to do it one at a time. You're an accomplice, and you own the actions of those other people because you agreed to be with them."

AG Downs advances in his PowerPoint presentation and shows a diagram of three gears turning together- one says riot, another says assault and a third says murder. He then continues his argument.

"The takeover was planned. Witness Curtis Demby says Dwayne Staats came to him before with a plan in progress. Curtis Demby says Dwayne Staats said he planned it. Assuming he was trying to help his friend, he said it was to be nonviolent. All along, this was planned to take those people down, no matter what it took. They had masks, gloves, weapons, shanks."

AG Downs then plays a clip of Jarreau Ayers' phone call with his sister from prior evidence. The section of the call that was played had to do with going to commissary, and contained thee N- word multiple times as well as motherfucker. He continued arguing.

"Jarreau Ayers tried to tell you this was a peaceful protest- that's all he knew. That phone call tells you it's a different story. They were conversing about it- saying 'we were gonna give everybody one more chance to go to the store' It was the Super Bowl- they wanted to watch- if it was before, they would have lockdown, go to the SHU. The plan was to do it after- his sister would get him money.

Jarreau Ayers thought it was funny to get peanut butter and crackers when planning a violent takeover. He said 'we,' meaning him and the others. When things went bad, they would have commissary. There was testimony about recruiting lifers- some with short time, [like] Roman Shankaras and Cut. There was preparation- Ms. May said in her testimony that the items she saw were stitched. She said she was treated better than anyone else, cared for better than anyone else.

In no way did that make it right- a woman over 60, I won't say her age, sitting in a chair all night long- it was flooded, you heard testimony about socks, going to the bathroom. That is nothing anybody wants to have happen in their life.

They were barricading doors, covering windows, threatening maintenance workers. In the testimony there were different perspectives and views on what was happening. They tried to block the C.O.s' view, block their entry. The maintenance men testified that they were upset because it was quiet, it was eerie. They threatened Dwayne Staats with spray, and told the coworkers to get into the basement- it wasn't their job to face whatever was there.

AG Downs then played a clip of Ayers on the negotiations. It was a section where he was talking about opening the door and saying they were being rushed by people in the yard. He is heard saying *'we ain't trying to see nobody get hurt.'*

"In the negotiations, there was the threat of violence. In Jarreau Ayers' testimony, he was mad because he was trying to do the right thing.

If Sergeant Floyd was already in the closet, there was someone already hurt- what he did make clear was if it's his life or some other MF's life he's choosing himself.

Sergeant Weaver's evidence; 126 inmates, some who committed crime. There was DNA. They tested for fingerprints. DNA is good, but if there's no explanation of why it got there.

Obadiah Miller's DNA was found in the mop closet. He lived on C Tier, he had access to the mop closet.

*Lauren Rothwell (*expert witness from DFS- Delaware's department of forensic science, who analyzed DNA in this case) *said it was there, but can't say for how long. It was a contaminated crime scene.*

There was four to five inches of water, mixed with blood from the attacks. There were clothes mixed up and burned. People had run of the building for hours. This case was not what the witnesses said. It was the largest crime scene DFS had ever examined, but very little found was of significance.

Royal Downs took a deal. He was a convicted murderer out of Maryland. The evidence is Royal Downs' roll was negotiations. He was all over that radio until he left.

Early on, Royal Downs gave information to investigators. On February 2 he made clear that he wouldn't talk long.

On February 15 he was interviewed at the infirmary- he explained his role, admitted to things. He informed that he tried to warn Sergeant Floyd in advance- he tried to fling that kite out of the tier. He said 'Ruck'- Jarreau Ayers- was his companion.

AG Downs then went over Royal Downs' mention of various others in his testimony.

Sergeant Floyd found his final resting place in the Sergeant's office. Because Royal Downs is a cooperating co-defendant, take great care and suspicion in viewing his testimony.

People taking a deal may try to minimize their involvement and shift blame to everyone else. These cases should be examined with more care. If they are reliable, then they are more so than other witnesses. Examine the evidence (with an eye toward its) corroboration with Royal Downs' testimony. He knew the takeover was planned. He knew it was for the Super Bowl.

Roman Shankaras sent the kite regarding the murder of Sergeant Floyd. He knew that knowledge would get him out of the SHU- maybe not out of prison. Others corroborate the testimony of Twin [Deric Forney] being involved. They saw him in the building putting a mask on, in B Tier attacking Officer Wilkinson.

AG Downs then listed witnesses' comments regarding people with nicknames, saying these are things that corroborate the testimony of Royal Downs. Then quoted from the kite attributed to Roman Shankaras.

"The rest was injuries inflicted during mop wringer action." Witness Henry Anderson said he was asleep, then he saw the mask off of Obadiah Miller.

AG Downs then reviews on bullet points of his PowerPoint page H.J.

Anderson's testimony about every incarcerated person named in the case. Abdul-Hafid As-Salafi said he was on the B Tier phone. Sergeant Weaver said he couldn't find that phone call- does that mean he wasn't?

This was a traumatic, disturbing experience for everybody. Royal Downs said that at 4:30am, he left. Regarding As-Salafi, if he's lying, if he's making it up to ingratiate himself with the state, that has to be one of the stupidest lies that anyone has told. Everyone knows phone calls are recorded- so he's lying, or he's mistaken.

"Richard McCane said a few people saw Obadiah Miller with the mask off. He saw Dwayne Staats throw bloody gloves in a trash can. He said he saw things through the door- he was questioned regarding using a mirror- at first he said he looked out, then he read what he said in his statement, that he used a mirror. He was mistaken. This was something that was a disturbing experience."

AG Downs then recapped the testimony of Antonio Guzman, including all the incarcerated people he named and what he said they did. He did the same with the testimony of Larry Sartin and Wade Smith.

"Eugene Wiggins testified about leaving. He testified about hearing 'jokers gotta stand up.' He also said he heard 'Floyd's done- he's cooked.' This is more than just a phrase to say dead evidence said Sergeant Floyd's body was burned because inmates were throwing burning things in on him."

AG Downs then recapped the testimony of Melvin Williams in the same fashion as others.

"Michael Rodriguez- he testified about an interaction in the yard- 'some inmates in C Tier, 'they're fucking the police up.' He testified that Jarreau Ayers told him 'shut the fuck up, or we'll do the same thing to you.'"

AG Downs' then listed what Michael Rodriguez testified about others. He advances his PowerPoint and sums up witness testimony against Jarreau Ayers- every line has what a state witness said about Ayers. He does the same for Deric Forney and Staats.

"Royal Downs gave lots of names of who he went into the building with, same as As-Salafi.

Andrew Sulner, the forensic document examiner's testimony was not very controversial. He verified the writers of the kites as Roman Shankaras and Dwayne Staats. The defense mentioned DNA.

There was testimony saying that they didn't find it on things, that there was contamination. Defense counsel for Deric Forney, Mr. Gifford asked witnesses if the police showed them photos of weapons and if they could identify which was used on Floyd.

Anyone would be hard-pressed to associate a shank with anyone. The defense's witness- DeShawn Drumgo wanted people to know he was there by waving to the camera in the yard by the infirmary. Did he alert the C.O.? He testified 'Why would I do that? Why would I cooperate with the police?' He made clear he wasn't happy with the state, he wasn't happy with his conviction, and he was appealing.

Luis Clarke testified he was out in the yard with Jarreau Ayers, and William "Bart" Lewis gave testimony about asking Jarreau Ayers to leave. The judge will talk to you about assessing witness credibility. DeShawn Drumgo, he doesn't like the police a little bit.

Clark and Lewis are 'close personal friends' of Jarreau Ayers. Dwayne Staats' witness Leroy McCoy testified that As-Salafi could not have seen anything he saw because he was in the cell the entire time with his celly and him.

DeShawn Drumgo was outside at this time. None of the witnesses have had completely consistent stories. It's a fluid situation. There are inconsistencies with the As-Salafi phone call. Royal Downs left at 4:30am.

Did Richard McCain look down the hall with a mirror? Use your common sense. This is what happens when people see things. They describe what it looks like to them, which is different from others.

Attorney Downs then gave an anecdote about friends who went camping and experienced a thunderstorm and flash flood, and how the husband gave a different account from the wife.

"They see what they see and they know what they know, and sometimes the little details lose their way."

The defendants testified for themselves. Jarreau Ayers said he wanted to help the inmates with medical problems. He said he didn't assault, kidnap or murder anyone. The evidence suggests that as an accomplice, he is liable. He admits he might have ordered lockerboxes to be slid out, and that's significant.

Jarreau Ayers will tell you as much of the truth as he wants to tell you. For example, he said he knew who else was involved, but wouldn't tell. He explained his phone call to his sister, he described the reality of the situation, but this was more than a peaceful protest.

Dwayne Staats said he didn't assault or murder anyone. He said 'Anyone else did anything, that's on them.' He admits to engaging with Ms. May, but not C.O. Wilkinson or C.O. Smith, or Sergeant

Floyd. Would someone who organized a takeover, who recruited and got it is going not know what happened?

He was negotiating for the letter of intent while Sergeant Floyd bled to death. Deric Forney testified he only started to be called 'Twin' after this incident- that's significant because on February 28 he gave a statement that no one calls him that. [State witness, nickname of] Lat said he was in the building, with a mask, planning to attack C.O. Wilkinson.

The question on February 28 was not a throwaway question. The evidence would suggest Deric Forney knew 'Twin' was involved. You heard witnesses say that not a lot of people knew [each other's] government names. 'I don't know his real name- I know him as..' When Deric Forney discussed 'Twin,' this was a little separation he wanted from this case."

AG Downs wrapped up his closing arguments.

Chapter 16

Jarreau Ayers began his closing argument shortly after Attorney Downs. Despite the fact that he was not an attorney or had any legal training, he delivered a powerful closing statement.

"This is out of the ordinary. Thank you, Your Honor- from the very beginning it seemed if Your Honor did two things- keep the situation impartial, so pro se defendants felt inclusive in what was going on. That was all I could ask.

Mr. Collins [standby counsel for Ayers]-,Mr. Vieth [standby counsel for Staats], Mr. Gifford [defense counsel for D. Forney], especially Mr. Gifford with the technicalities, he had to step up and hold the integrity from the standpoint.

And the integrity in the courtroom- y'all, the jury watched me like I watched y'all. You tried to be impartial; you took notes on all of it. My opening statements, I feel hold true right now.

These are cases built on the backs of individuals desperate to go home. There were deals made to go on the stand. The testimony, more on point, Antonio Guzman-, he is housed with witnesses against me. When did he realize that he would receive no deal? 1 week ago.

While picking the jury for this trial he thought he would have a deal. February 2017 until a week prior to now, he believed he would get a deal. I've never believed in something for 2 years and then stopped believing in 7 days.

The DNA evidence. I spoke on that because it didn't identify anyone. The state's accomplice theory likens it to touching things in your house. The reality is common sense.

If a glove with DNA and prints on the inside and outside matched me, they would parade it every chance they got to show it. Because there was no DNA attached, the state tells you, 'DNA doesn't matter that's the common sense in that.'

Ayers shows State's Exhibit #330 and continues his closing statement.

"The picture book. Page 2, picture 7. As-Salafi. Walter Smith. I know him as Umar.

He said he saw the assault on Smith. The assailant was wearing a mask, and a hoodie. They had my body shape. There are 5 other witnesses. None of them said Jarreau Ayers attacked Floyd.

Also Floyd was attacked in a different direction from me. Lieutenant Sennett said on the stand, never in 13 years did he see an inmate run TO a Code 1. As-Salafi testified he ran, and that he saw it in a different direction.

But his phone call doesn't matter to the state's case. Mine did. Lat's phone call- they found that. They can't find As-Salafi's, so that doesn't matter.

I'm a pro se defendant. I have every phone call from January 1 through March 31 of 2017, and they can't find As-Salafi.

"Larry Sartin, I know him as Jaybird. He testified under oath that he looked in my face when I called in yard. I pulled out the statement he gave- not only did he not see, he only heard a voice. He said 'I don't know who it was, I only heard a voice, it's not like I saw out the door, I didn't see.'

'Being rushed', the state supports that- at the same time, they want you to believe everything they say about the co-Ds. 'Now that I did see it, I said that.' He didn't see it because it didn't happen. You're gonna see it, we'll go through it. Wade Smith.

I got emotional. I got heated. Mr. 'I Don't Recall.' For instance, how he said I wouldn't let him go.

I showed him his statement- 'it was insinuated,' but it says right here in the statement; then he changes his story to Bart. I don't know, it was cool when Bart said this, but I put Bart on the stand- yeah, that's my friend, but it has nothing to do with someone lied.

I bring him up here, they try to say that doesn't matter. About seeing me outside- Bart, DeShawn Drumgo, Luis Clark- 'they're my friends, don't believe them.'

Royal Downs and Lat said they saw me outside. People for me and the state also said that. And DeShawn Drumgo is my cousin, not Luis Clark..

"Eugene Wiggins- he testified he actually saw my face saying come in. In his statement, he said, 'I don't know nothing- I can't say because I didn't see, I only heard a voice.'

The detective asked 'you know stuff but don't want to identify?' and he said 'no, I don't know, I didn't see.' On the stand, he said 'I saw Jarreau Ayers."

In the statement in the courthouse, not a rush statement, to the DA he said 'I only heard the voice, a gut feeling it's Jarreau, but I could be wrong.' And he said on the stand I looked him in the face. The state knows that. But, if I didn't tell you that, they weren't gonna tell you all that.

Burn aka Eugene Wiggins, his second statement about leaving. He never said in his statement that he asked me about leaving. He attributed every detail of the conversation to me, but in the statement he said it was Royal Downs. Now I'm facing life in the hole. I could be locked down in the hole, 23 and 1. A life sentence its consequences. He lied, his statement showed he lied.

Antonio Guzman said 'Ayers called us in- I seen Ayers, no mask on.' Everyone said a mask, but bigger, stronger than that. There was a detailed account in February. There was testimony about 2 calls in from rec/yard, one from Floyd, one from an inmate.

In statement #1 he said he went in with the initial attack, and that was how he saw the attacks. He named names, he names who did it. When it's time for these individuals to go to trial, they'll use those statements. What that means is 'he wasn't outside like he said he was'.

He said 'and I was outside.' Sergeant Weaver asked him about the attack, and he said 'damn right I stayed outside.' Sergeant Weaver asked who was the inmate? 'Ruck.' Was he wearing a mask? There was no context in the statement-, 'this is what you said, you were caught in a lie before the jury, and here's the paperwork to show it.'

Antonio Guzman, and Luis Clark- asked 'who were you with?' 'L Dog.' It's not like I wanted to call these people. But there's a code of ethics-, when you send paperwork to jails, so they don't think someone's getting called to Delaware to testify against people.

About leaving, about no kidnapping charge about inmates. It's crazy I feel I have to testify against it.

The reality is its a lie. Every lie, every inconsistency, every contradiction- I said in the beginning, whether I need to fight this charge or not, I will do what I gotta do.

Witness Williams(Lump). The DA was absolutely wrong. He never said on the stand that 'Ruck was opening the door to let people in our out.' What he said was 'Ruck let me out.'

He was on the medical wave. He told you all what happened. There was no kidnapping charge about inmates, but I have to tell you. I let him out, he never saw me with weapons, with a mask or assaulting anyone.

Michael Rodriguez, Lat. I grew up with him. He testified he came out- y'all gotta judge his credibility, but he testified that I was outside when he was, and what As-Salafi said.

It was clear people I had love for were inside- what is going on? I asked Lat, and he said 'it's messy.'

Their witness said I was outside. He pivoted and said I spoke about killing someone, 'I forgot.' You talked to the prosecution four times and this never came up? 400 pages of talking is a lot of talking. He never said I did something to someone, or that I called people in. I didn't 'threaten to kill people.' He said 'I asked Royal Downs to leave and Royal Downs said come to Ayers'- we know what you're trying to do. On the stand, he said 'Diamond had to ask me.'

To this day it's hard to fathom why he popped up with that. Royal Downs. Yeah, everybody know him. There's not much I can say about me and him that was not already said.''

He is engaged to testify against everybody. He's someone I used to deal with. He talk forever, but, 'I don't know why Ruck was charged,' don't pay attention to that. 'Ruck was outside,' that doesn't matter. 'Twin did this, Smoke does that.'

He said the day before, and then 'Ruck helped plan.''

The star witness said I found out the day before- someone said it's going down. If I had knowledge, that is completely different than planning.

I knew, I never lied, I found out the night before. I was telling my sister- I found out the next morning it's going down. I knew it was going to be real, no question- I never hid it on the stand. I wasn't planning, helping or doing those things.

The star witness said that, but only pay attention to the negative. I am charged with planning the takeover. Not one person said that. Not one person said that I was with a group of people, that morning- As-Salafi, even, but we can move on from him.

Five witnesses all said I was not involved except As-Salafi. I didn't have weapons, I didn't have masks. This is my fight, what I'm up against.

I believed I understood reasonable doubt, presumed innocent, and a fight for freedom. Now that I looked at it, Mr. Gifford explained something different.

It might be how Jarreau Ayers feels, that I have the right, a right people die for, to have reasonable doubt, to be presumed innocent, to have transparency and clarity.

It bothered me until now, that the only reason I got this. It never computed in my mind that I was afforded that type of justice. To sit at the table, tell my story, to have a proper defense. It happened like it was supposed to.

It never dawned on me that that applied to what I thought: every contradiction on the stand that I proved, the only thing I had to fight against was that no one would fight for me.

While finishing his argument, Jarreau Ayers made a demonstration of his point with a cup of water and black ink. He drizzled the ink into the water and showed how it changed the contents of the cup.

"The contradictions took away from what Mr. Gifford said, what I was afforded. Now you're told to disregard the contradictions, and what is left is the justice I have. The same justice before they dumped all those contradictions in there."

Chapter 17

While both Staats and Ayers represented themselves in the proceedings, Benjamin Gifford, was the defense counsel for Deric Forney. He delivered his closing arguments shortly after Ayers.

"Good afternoon, all. There's not a lot for me to talk about- we've done what is important. The state is attempting to convince you about the crime of riot which went on from 10am February 1 to 5am February 2. Their definition is not right.

The evidence supports the conclusion that the riot started around 10am and lasted approximately 30 minutes, not that it continues happening until they retake the building. That's it, now a new phase. Hostage negotiation, kidnapping. There's a relatively discrete set of crimes- 5 or more. Riot, conspiracy- can this be grouped with it?- assaults on C.O.s Smith, Wilkinson and Sergeant Floyd, kidnapping of those, and Sergeant Floyd's murder.

The state charged with 3 counts of murder- how can they be found guilty of intentional murder when Dr. Collins [the medical examiner] testified, and AG Downs reminded you this morning, that they don't know who gave the death blow?

That doesn't sound like there was intention. They didn't stab to kill, they didn't hit to kill. He was in the closet. He bled out. That's why he died. I don't know that anyone committed murder.

The strongest charge is murder in the commission of a felony. Sergeant Floyd may have died because of other crime, but not riot. You heard Dr. Collins testify that he had superficial wounds, and that he could have been saved.

The kidnapping charges; injuries occurred around 10am. Then Sergeant Floyd was held for ten to fourteen hours. Had they let him go, released him as a hostage, he would probably he here today. That didn't happen. The kidnapping maybe led to his death. Had the state said he died with the kidnapping, that could be trouble, but the riot?

Look at the evidence- Disorderly conduct, conspiracy to commit assault, not felony murder during kidnapping- it's too broad. Just because the state charges someone with something, doesn't mean it isn't right to look at it critically.

"The investigation. Sergeant Weaver. What WAS this investigation? First- what didn't they do? There were lots of answers on direct examination about what happened- people live there, there's DNA everywhere.

Sergeant Weaver said it was like a home. AG Downs said DNA is only useful in stranger cases, so in prison it would not be useful.

I'll offer a story-, a man is suspected of killing his wife. There's a gun on the floor. AG Downs might say there are the husband's fingerprints on the gun, but don't give that weight- he lives there, it may be his gun.

The 'tainted scene' mindset- from day 1, why didn't Detective Cresto dust everything? If this was 'the biggest case in DFS history', as Lauren Rothwell said. It doesn't add up.

"Detective Cresto collected evidence. This gem," Gifford said, presenting an early state exhibit. A diagram of C Building with circles large and small and numbers showing where evidence items were said to be found.

"We haven't seen this in a while. State's #4, it's 'not to scale', that's how this was described. The care they showed while creating this is the care they gave the whole investigation. They didn't tell you they

cut off half the building, they moved things. They didn't testify to their independent thoughts, they couldn't remember.

This was poor, shoddy investigative work. It piles up during the investigation.

In week 3, Sergeant Weaver- he never showed you, he made this big blow-up. There was talk about cost. It was a big case, there was a death of a correctional officer. Thinking of cost, when you didn't test the murder weapons- how much did it cost to show you this schematic for 1 day?

Sergeant Floyd didn't deserve to die. It was a tragedy. So is this investigation. Sergeant Floyd didn't deserve this investigation, either. Are you serious? Only witnesses. No bloody gloves, blood all over the C.O.s, they were beaten by people in the building, there was a cut on someone's hand- they didn't test any of that?

Bloody clothes- the detail of this investigation, the chain of custody. You have photos for one officer and not another- you did nothing, so the state held back about the other officer's clothes.

If they're hiding something like that from you. I asked Sergeant Weaver about the quantum of evidence necessary to charge someone. He said 2 people. Two inmates- not Ms. May, not the firefighters, not the C.O.s. 'Beyond a reasonable doubt'- there is no number, but it's higher than 1.6%. Two inmate witnesses is less than that. All the evidence, plus two witnesses.

We are asked to ignore the same number of witnesses who say definitively that no, Deric Forney was not involved. Lat and Umar say they saw Deric Forney in the corridor by the barbershop. Anthony Morrow was on the phone- he says 'no,' 'I know Deric Forney,' 'he's my brother in Christ,' 'we're friends,' 'it wasn't him.'

But ignore that- we don't like that testimony. Anthony Morrow was asked by Ms. Warner about recognizing someone in a mask. He said 'I wouldn't recognize you if you were in a mask.'

What is it about the other witnesses who say they can recognize someone in a mask and Anthony Morrow can't? Why pick and choose?"

Attorney Gifford tells a story about how he was "prepping with notes, pages and pages of contradictions," and he brought up Forrest Gump, which was on the TV in the background.

"A historical drama of things that happened- they filmed Tom Hanks and inserted him into footage. We know it's a work of fiction. That's what these witnesses are doing- taking things that happened and putting people in there like Forrest Gump.

On the tiers there is a corridor about 6 feet wide. Someone testified that if M. Rodriguez was walking down B Tier, why didn't Anthony Morrow see him?

If As-Salafi was coming- and that's a pretty big 'if'- he didn't see the attacks, but a random inmate saw, he definitely wasn't there. There was testimony that it's a closed space, and everybody knows each other. From 10am February 1 to 5am February 2, did they plan what to do after?

To think, they planned a takeover and attack and never thought about how to get away with it? What crime did they do? Why the police?

To believe they didn't talk-, 'let's say this person did it, people don't know, we'll say he did it, he's only been in the building four weeks'. Royal Downs, and Lat- his little brother. Leaders of men. As-Salafi- he went on for 40 minutes about how he's respected. He's a leader of men. You don't think people talked?

AG Downs talked about the river. I'm not sure why it matters, but if it did, inconsistencies may matter, but thunder at 12:15? What are we supposed to do with that story? People disagree- at least one is wrong, maybe both. They said they were in C Building. They didn't say they weren't. Did they see what they saw?

At the beginning I said there was a wall of reasonable doubt, and it was the state's responsibility to tear that down. Unreasonable doubt would be 'someone drove to Vaughn and broke in and killed Sergeant Floyd,' 'Deric Forney wasn't in the building, so no crime'. You don't replace common sense- it's good to use.

Go with the probabilities- what is more likely? That's not the standard here- think of the preponderance of the evidence in a car accident. Someone has to pay- so you decide where the preponderance of the evidence lies.

If you think Deric Forney is probably guilty? If you think he's highly probably guilty? That's not enough. The standard is clear and convincing evidence and highly probable. This is what has to be done before taking someone's children away [for example]. If the best you can say its clear and convincing, it's 'not guilty.' Reasonable doubt, use your common sense.

You're told 'ignore the inconsistencies, contradictions.' I was gonna say 'ignore the potential benefits,' but, It doesn't matter regarding the state's benefits- hope springs eternal. A habitual offender looking for commutation- Henry Anderson believes the state helped him, so he helps them.

Anthony Morrow said C Building and the SHU are hell on earth. The DOC controls everything about people's lives while they're in prison. Who they see, who they talk to, when they come out of a 6 x 6 cell. Will it be 18 hours a day or 1? It's all the DOC. A correctional officer died- in that community, that's a big deal. It's a tragedy, they lost a brother.

Do you think it's possible that inmates who testify and the DOC thinks it's possible they helped the prosecution, that the DOC helped them? Send them upstate, help with their return.

Is the Delaware prison system so awful you'd like to get out? Deric Forney said he didn't do it- he was in his cell, he comforted his celly, they ate food.

He hung around the good cook guy, and he prayed. He wanted to make sure Ms. May was okay, and he didn't think he could ask to leave. There were lists of things people did- where's Deric at?

How's he involved and no one sees until after? The only thing we heard is he went to someone's cell for a cinnamon roll, because he was hungry.

He is the only indicted inmate we don't hear about until later- he told you he wasn't involved. Is there a possibility, or a probability, that he's telling the truth under oath?

If not, you have to acquit- it's required under the law. You heard questions from the state, in the cross-examination of Deric Forney. The story wasn't full of crap, it was used to bolster other stories. 'Ordered to come in.' There was lots of focus on 'order'/'not order,' and I am not sure why. There is no such thing as 'undecided'; if you're undecided, the state didn't it's.

Same with lingering questions. We can point to certain things- if it's possible, it's probably not true. If it's probably not true, that means not guilty. Even if you don't believe it, even if you think it is unreasonable- like the hypothetical break-in to the prison to murder Sergeant Floyd or Hawaii doesn't exist- that's reasonable doubt. AG Downs had a PowerPoint.

He went on about Jarreau Ayers, lines, and lines and lines. Dwayne Staats, lines and lines and lines. For Deric Forney, there were 4 lines, and my grandma could read them from the back. She's 88 years old. That's the evidence. He's innocent. He said it. Thank you for your time- I ask that you return the only verdict possible against Mr. Forney and that is not guilty.

Chapter 18

On November 20th, the verdict was handed down for the first trial group.

Dwayne Staats is found guilty on two of the three counts of first degree murder he was charged with. Staats and Jarreau Ayers are found guilty of riot, conspiracy, and assault of correctional officers and kidnapping. Deric Forney is found not guilty on all charges.

After the verdict, Dwayne Staats addressed the courts from a pre drafted letter. The words were defiant. Staats had not spoken much during the trial and when he did, his arrogance were apparent.

It was clear that he took pride in being able to convince other prisoners to revolt. Staats' was already serving a life sentence without parole, and had nothing to lose.

"My goal was to do something to expose this place to where the public and government would take notice. Guess I got their attention," he said.

"A lot of stuff wasn't being addressed until that happened...I just wanted to put the attention on the prison because everybody was like oblivious to what was going on."

While Staats believed the takeover was 'absolutely necessary,' he says the murder of Floyd was not a part of the plan.

"I mean, it's a tragedy that he died, but that wasn't the plan...I gotta eat that because that's what happened in my plan." "Every time I see the news article or hear about it on the radio, I be like 'damn, all this happened because of one thought in this brain of mine,'" the letter read.

"Honestly, it feels surreal knowing that everything that transpired started from one thought...now I truly understand the concept of the tree is inside the seed. If shit hit the fan and my number is called, I'm going pro se. Eff a suit, I'm wearing a T-shirt and DOC pants. This is gonna be epic."

"I didn't wear no mask or nothing, so it was a high probability that I was going to get indicted, and I wasn't ducking at it or nothing like that."

"I put deep thought, this ain't no rash decision. You living and surviving, feel this stuff, so it's like a deep contemplation, so then when you see it manifest in reality, it feel surreal sometimes 'cause you like, this actually happened, years and years I've been around people...for me it was just time," he said.

"For me, it wasn't really about the violence." "I didn't kill nobody, I didn't even assault nobody. Am I capable? Probably, anybody's capable of violence. You got 10-year-olds committing violent acts, that wasn't part of the plan. The takeover, of course there would be some assaults and that stuff, but my hands? Nah."

"Those who understand that the uprising needed to happen knew that shit was going to get worse before it got better. I guess that's with anything we're fighting for...that's what the struggle is...keep pushing, pushing, pushing. You might get pushed back, but that's the hope--that one day it's going to get better."

Dwayne Staats refused to identify six inmates directly involved in attacks on correctional officers—like co defendant Jarreau Ayers.

"I had a rough two years man, I'm mentally deteriorated. Me and Mr. Ayers got the same condition...I don't remember," he said.

"You can dress it up any way you want to. I'm telling you, I stated if I was gonna go that route, I would've corroborated with that all. If I was gonna do all that--point people out--cooperate with the state, I'd have done it when you came in and talked to me."

"I guess this whole thing, right now, it's just me taking responsibility for the uprising. I'mma own it," said Staats.

SENTENCING

Dwayne Staats, sentenced to two life sentences in prison plus 153 years for his conviction on 2 counts of Murder First Degree, Riot, 2 counts of Assault First Degree, 4 counts of Kidnapping First Degree, and Conspiracy Second Degree.

Jarreau Ayers, sentenced to 123 years for his conviction on Riot, 2 counts of Assault First Degree, and 4 counts of Kidnapping First Degree, and Conspiracy Second Degree.

Deric Forney was found not guilty on all charges.

Chapter 19

Jury selection for the second trial group began on January 7th. The defendants were Obadiah Miller, John Bramble, Kevin Berry, and Abednego Baynes.

Each faced murder charges for the death of Correctional Officer Steven Floyd as well as assault, riot, kidnapping and conspiracy to riot.

Unlike the previous defendants, the inmates had attorneys represent them, Andrew Witherell, Anthony Figliola, and Tom Pedersen.

Andrew Witherell, who represented Berry, says, *"It's going to come down to credibility of the witnesses who take that stand, and each one of you I'm going to ask, please, please listen and make a judgment with respect to any biases, concerns, trickery, or whatever they expect to get out of this trial."*

Attorney Tom Pedersen, who represented Bramble, took that one step further, saying the prosecution's case rests on the *"testimony of snakes"* - in a declaration that drew an objection, a rarity in opening statements.

"You're going to hear a dizzying array of contradiction--contradictions between each individual witness and what they have said on the different times they were interviewed, and contradictions between what one witness for the state says as opposed to the other witness." Did these witnesses see the same events? Are you to rely on those witnesses, those stories, and those contradictions

to return a verdict of guilty? I submit to you there's no way humanly possible you will be able to do that" he said.

Pedersen also brought up the credibility issue and asked the jury to use common sense.

"The kind of common sense that says an inmate doesn't come to court to testify unless he wants something in return. It's the kind of common sense folks that tells you that when someone says different things over the course of different interviews--that person's not to be trusted. It's the kind of common sense that if you're lost and you ask 10 different people for directions home, and they tell you 10 different ways to get home, you're still lost," said Pedersen.

"When you see a poisonous snake on the ground you don't pick him up and put him in the pot."

The attorneys for inmates on trial asked the prosecution to look beyond the stigma of incarceration and insist on the presumption of innocence in a case that brings about two challenges.

"First, can we really give a presumption of innocence to someone who's already in jail? We're all human, we know what the instructions tell us, but there's a human side to us that says, 'Well someone's already in jail they must be bad people; they must've done something wrong'...as we sit here right now, Mr. Bramble is as innocent of these charges as both you and I," Pedersen said.

"Second challenge—when you look at this case overall, is it easier to sometimes say, 'Hey, if we got this wrong, if we're relying on people who we otherwise wouldn't rely it is it OK because the people we're making mistakes about are already in jail?' Are they less worthy of us doing this the right way? Are they less worthy of us relying on good, sound evidence because they're inmates? Would you be satisfied with the quality of prosecution that you're going to hear if Mr. Bramble was the valedictorian of the charter school? Because those two people, the

valedictorian at the charter school and Mr. Bramble deserve the same treatment." said Pedersen.

Attorney Cleon Cauley, who represented Baynes, said his client did not take part in any planning of the incident or the attacks.

"Simply being present isn't enough. When you look at the evidence, you'll see that no DNA comes back to my client, no fingerprints come back to my client, the state's star witness will tell you that my client was not involved."

Tony Figliola, who represented Miller, claimed his client did not participate in the riot because he didn't want to jeopardize his impending release in October of 2019.

"He was not a long-timer, he was not one of the guys that had nothing to lose by causing a prison uprising. He was a friend of some of the organizers, he got dragged into this by other inmates because of his association with those individuals," said Figliola.

Cauley called it a *"snap judgement"* on the part of the state that led to his client being charged.

Figliola called it *"selective prosecution."*

"There's 126 inmates in the C building--only 18 are charged. The state talks about direct evidence and circumstantial evidence. What's the direct evidence? Testimony from the individuals that weren't charged. That's their 'direct' evidence. Some of them come forward within a day; some say, 'I want a lawyer;' some of 'em go two or three times until they get a lawyer—they're looking for a deal," Figliola claimed.

On February 19, their trial wrapped up without any convictions. Abednego Baynes and Kevin Berry were acquitted on all counts.

For John Bramble or Obadiah Miller, the jury could not reach a verdict on the riot and assault charges and acquitted the two men of the rest of their charges.

At the time, the state did not mention of they were going to pursue another trial for Bramble and Miller.

Chapter 20

This Letter is a confession on my behalf to clear my conscience in regards to the Vaugan uprising that took place on 2/1/17. I regret waiting this late to confess because my actions have resulted in the unjustly indictment of 13 of my codefendants. I am no longer live with the guilt and 13 others shouldnt suffer behind my selfishness. Royal Downs was my celly and he and I along with 5 others planned the uprisings Royal Downs used to always tell me how he wanted to go back to Maryland and how fed up he was with the way prisoners were being treated He's been planning the takeover for a few months and I became part of the plan since he trusted me. His exact words were "the administration already think I'm the Boss in here so I/we mind as well show them whats up." I allowed him to manipulate me with Revolutionary literature and when the time came I acted. On the morning of 2/1/17 after Sgt. Floyd called yard, myself and 5 others stormed the bldg. while hiding in the oncoming rush of others (inmates) entering the building. This first CO I came into contact with was floyd. I pulled out my shank and stabbed him in the arm while others went and attacked the other co's. After stabbing Floyd multiple times in different places I quickly picked up a mop ringer and when he started to retreat I hit him in the head with it. When he fell others jumped on him and began assaulting him as well. While swinging the Mop ringer I believe I may have unknowingly hit some light skinned guy in his arm or hand because I could see it bleeding while he was holding away. Once all 3 cos were subdued we put them in closets, put the counselor on G-Tier and started negotiating. In the middle of all of this from, I saw Corey Smith, trying to sneak into the basement with the maintenance workers. Since the maintenance workers didn't help him he then walked outside. After that I went outside while still masked up and told everyone to come inside. Afterwards I went to my celly Royal Downs and told him everyone (CO's) were secured and thats when he said "we have to make an example out of one of em."

It just so happened to be Floyd that day. Throughout the rest of the day I along with 2 others continued to assault Floyd. After a while he just stopped moving so we put him in the sgt's office and I threw burnt objects on top of him. I won't name the other 4 individuals who helped me throughout the day because I won't be the cause of the true perpitrators being indicted. I know for a fact that Luis Sierra, Obadiah Miller, John Band, ..., Alejandro Rodriguez-Ortiz, Pedro Chavez, Kevin Berry, Jarris Mathis, Robert Hernandez, Corey Smith, Jonathan Rodriguez, Lawrence Michael and Roman Shankaras had nothing to do with the Riot, Conspiracy, Kidnappn Assault and Murder on 2/1/17 at J.T.V.C.C. I'm sorry for my actions

Kelly _____ 11/21/18

In the early morning hour of November 22, 2018, Kelly Gibbs, age 30, took his life by hanging in his prison cell at Howard R Young Correctional Institution in Wilmington, Delaware.

Two days before this, he signed a plea agreement in which he took responsibility for his role in the February 1, 2017, riot. Prison Officials found his body as well as two suicide notes. One to a family member and the other in which he admitted his actions during the uprising, and it exonerated 13 of the men who were facing murder tied to the death of Correctional Officer Steven Floyd. Mr. Gibbs letter reads:

"This letter is a confession on my behalf to clear my conscience in regards to the Vaughn uprising that took place on 2/1/2017. I regret waiting this late to confess because my actions have resulted in the unjustly indictment of 13 of my Co Defendant's.

I can no longer live with the guilt and 13 others shouldn't suffer behind my selfishness. Royal Downs was my celly and he and I along with 5 others planned the uprisings. Royal Downs used to always tell me how he wanted to go back to Maryland and how fed up he was with the prisoners were being treated. He's been planning a takeover for a few months and I became a part of the plan since he trusted me. His exact words were "the administration already think I'm the Boss in here & I/We mind as well show them whats up". I allowed him to manipulate me with Revolutionary literature and when the time came I acted. On the morning of 2/1/17 after Sgt. Floyd called yard, myself and 5 others stormed the bldg while hiding in the oncoming rush of others(inmates) entering the building. This first CO I came into contact with was Floyd. I pulled back my shank and stabbed him in the arm while others went and attacked the other Co's. After stabbing Floyd multiple times in different places I quickly picked up a mop ringer and when he started to retreat I hit him in the head with it. When he fell others jumped on him and began assaulting him as well. While swinging the mop ringer I believe I may have unknowingly hit some lightskinned guy on his arm or hand because I could see it bleeding while he was walking away. Once all 3 Co's were subdued we put them in closets, put the counselor on B-Tier and started negotiating. In the middle of all of the Prog.

I saw Corey Smith trying to sneak into the basement with maintenance workers. Since the maintenance workers didn't help him he walked outside after that I went outside while all masked up and told everyone to come inside. Afterward I went to my celly Royal Downs and told him everyone(cos) were secured and that's when he said "We have to make an example out of one of em". It just so happened to be Floyd that day. Throughout the rest of the day I along with 2 others continued to assault Floyd. After a while he just stopped moving, so we put him in the Sgt's office and I threw burnt object on top of him. I won't name the other 4 individuals who helped me throughout the day because I won't be the cause of the true perpetrator's being indicted.

I know for a fact that Luis Sierra, Obadiah Miller, John Bramble, Abednego, Alejandro Rodrigues- Ortiz, Pedro Chairez, Kevin Berry, Janiis Mathis, Robert Hernandez, Corey Smith, Jonaton Rodrequez, Lawrence Micheals, and Roman Shankaras had nothing to do with the riot, Conspiracy, Kidnapping, Assault and Murder on 2/17/17 at J.T.V.C.C. I am sorry for my actions."

The letter is signed by Mr. Gibbs on 11/28/18. He was pronounced dead at 2:25 am.

The handwritten letter written by Gibbs was not immediately available. The contents of this document were kept from the public eye.

There is no doubt that Kelly Gibbs' claimed responsibility for the death of Sgt. Floyd as well as naming the state's Star Witness as a one of the men who planned, and actively participated in the riot.

As a result of the letter, 13 of the men charged with the murder of Sgt. Floyd, the riot, and the kidnapping were exonerated.

Chapter 21

Following the exoneration of the exonerated inmates, the inmates were immediately transferred to prisons outside of the state.

The receiving prisons immediately housed them in RRL (Restricted Release).

This means, plainly put, that despite the fact that they had been exonerated, they had still been ordered to stay in solitary confinement until they were released. The initial reasons given were related to a riot.

It was only after being challenged, and presenting supporting documentation for the facts, that the reasons were renamed as 'misconduct issues'.

Initially, Pennsylvania Governor Wolf and the Superintendent, Michael Zaken, supported and stood firm on the lie that the RRL status of the transferred inmates was due to riots. Moreover, all reviews and documentation support this as well.

As soon as legal action was threatened, the story changed completely. Mark DiAlesandro, Deputy Superintendent for Centralized Services, called me to explain the inmates' RRL status as a result of misconduct.

He later contradicted himself and stated that the inmates were immediately sent to Restricted Release from prison due to the riot. This is the case with all of the transferred prisoners. As of the date of this publication, the men that are still incarcerated remain in solitary confinement.

That is 23 hours every day locked inside their cell. Was justice really served?

Indefinite Solitary Confinement

Please note that I do not endorse any of the views in the following pages. Rather, I am giving each man a forum to speak their truth.

ALEJANDRO RODSIGUEZ-ORTIZ

My name is Alejandro Rodriguez-Ortiz of the Vaughn 17. Two months ago. I was transferred to Sci-Phoenix from Sci-Mahanoy to be put in a program called "The Intensive Management Unit".

This program was supposedly established to give us an avenue to get off of the "Restricted Release List", the one of the most austere security housing levels left in this country, Indefinite solitary confinement.

First of all, I was placed on this status without due process. I have no write-ups in Pennsylvania. My last significant issue in Delaware was in February 2014. I wasn't convicted of the events of the Vaughn Up Rise.

So administration has no way to justify this. Yet I was given any means to appeal their arbitrary decision. This housing for my comrades & I is strictly a means to punish us for crimes that they couldn't convict us in court for.

So they send us to a state that hasn't abolished this archaic, tortuous punishment known as solitary confinement. Now we've been in this "IMU" program for up to 3 months. You would think that the things that the state funded Sci-Phoenix to run like educational programs, rehab programs,etc would be running. There is nothing.

To date, we are told that no policy for the "IMU" has been written. We live in the "IMU" yet the "IMU" doesn't exist. For the last 72 hours, a couple dozen like-minded comrade & I have been on a hunger strike.

We haD some minor issues that we are in talks with handling in house.But our primary issue is that we have no "IMU" policy & procedure book. How to we grieve a program that doesn't exist?

How to do complete a program that never starts?We need to know what is actually expected of us & what we can expect from them.

We can't move forward until that basic element is established. We are not ending this movement until central office stops procrastinating & produces the program that the taxpayers have been paying for for the last few months. We aren't asking for anything but our basic rights.

Peace,   Only their tactics have changed. But white nationalism is alive and thriving. You see it every day in their laws and draconian police brutality. How many black and Brown brothers have to die at the hands of a predominately white police force?

How many families of Latin descent have to be separated? How many prisons have to be built? How many walls have to be erected?

The hate-mongering infests our nation at its core. That "legal" document I quoted earlier was written 500 years ago, yet it's still reflected in our society today.   Just because it's not laid out so cut and dry. Believe me, we are still living under the same colonial belief system that tried to destroy us back then.

They want to classify us as subhuman, barbaric, savage, illiterate, drug dealers, gang bangers, murderers. This image they want to portray reinforces their own rationalization that we need to be governed and controlled.

This gives them the moral and intellectual right to claim superiority. And then depict themselves as brave and courageous seekers of justice and freedom. But I say fuck their misconceived moral right from god.

We will outlast, out breed and overcome them on every level. They are the true savages that destroy and annihilate entire nations and cultures. They kill indiscriminately.

Everywhere the white man went he brought death and destruction. Stealing and raping the land of all its natural resources. They take our wealth and then subject us to the yoke. And when we struggle in poverty, they call us lazy.

Our children end up attending the worst school districts in the nation. And they call us illiterate. But they fail to recognize that the adversity and hate and pain we endure daily only makes us stronger, and more dangerous.

And one day in the near future they will awake in fear and feel our feet on the back of their necks! Solidarity, I was recently informed of Reverend Al Sharpton's visit to the city along with the speech he delivered on the lack of diversity within the state's judiciary branch. I in comradely with our people have felt the importance to acknowledge this moment.

To express my thoughts on the plight of those generations to come, who will ultimately be subjected to the torture of a broke antiqued racist system. A system that not only endorses the owning of human beings, but also the acquisition and financial capitalization of owning human beings called "Indentured Servitude".

A system that indulges in quid pro quo for retaliation. Publicly advocating for prison reform and humane conditions for those incarcerated, simply to appease its democratic base to secure votes!

Then, ultimately using taxpayers to turn around and ship inmates" Majority Black bodies" and those at the bottom of the social-economic ladder to be subjected to torture conditions in out-of-state prisons like me & my co-defendants'.

History tells us that there is nothing more important to a revolutionary change than "MOMENT"! If you are able to consciously identify & seize the MOMENT, then you can completely alter the trajectory to which those who capitalize off, of this evil system, wish for us to remain on.

I suggest that as a people our goal has to be to squeeze everything out of the MOMENT and not simply accept what they concede to us as a shallow victory that inevitably won't have any true effect on change.

Mrs. Tamika Montgomery- Reeves's appointment is a win for our people. President Barack Obama's election was a great historical victory for our people, yet the true change we sought to grab from the MOMENT slipped through our hands because every Pivotal bill he attempted to pass could have had a positive multi-generational impact on our communities' was denied by congress.

Therefore, while Reverend Al Sharpton's attack on the judiciary branch is an admirable first step, ultimately to have a true impact on this racist capitalistic disease that's breaking apart families & destroying our communities we have to apply this cure of diversity to every political branch of Delaware's bureaucracy.

Truthfully, before & after this is accomplished we have to demand transparency & integrity from our leaders and let them know they can no longer just deliver our votes to whomever they politically endorse. Simply being an orator of beautiful speeches will no longer be accepted they have to truly move out for the people! With visions of a Better future! Stay strong & Stay focused! All power is the people!!

Abdul Haqq

Dear Comrades:

For those of you who have shown support for the Vaughn17, I am sending you this message in order to express my appreciation and to commend you for the courage and work that you have done and continue to do for all prisoners suffering behind enemy lines.

Despite our short encounters of success, the fight against this unproductive, oppressive system is far from over! Not only is there a lot of work that needs to be done, but we have to remain diligent in our efforts to combat this system.

Speaking of the system, as you know, it is once again an election year. Politics play a pivotal role in how this country operates its systems.

I am not sure how many of you Brothers and Sisters believe in politics and voting, but for those of you who do not—you need to. As we all know, mass incarceration is a real thing that is affecting all races in this country, especially people of color.

In saying that, a lot of these politicians are now using mass incarceration as a stepping stool to win the Black and Latino vote. Therefore, all of you need to make sure that you have valid reasons on why you are voting for the politicians that you are voting for.

Whatever you do, please do not mistake the dialogue and charisma of a politician as a way of promise and capability, because this is nothing but a sales pitch to win your vote.

If you start to develop a good vibe from somebody, then make sure that you investigate them because it is wiser to base your vote on something you have actually investigated than on something that you feel. Remember, deception is real and politicians have a way of portraying images for the benefit of their personal agendas. In closing, continue to live the spirit of our ancestors and remain steadfast in our struggle against oppression and the prison state. Peace. In Solidarity, Your Brother In Struggle Abdul Haqq

DERICK FORNEY

Greetings People, 1st, I'd like to say that it is a blessing and my pleasure that I got to speak with you, the people. Because we the people make the difference. I pray that all is well with you and yours. And despite the current challenges and disadvantages that Vaughn17 prisoners and other prisoners who are on the RRL and/or trapped in the RHU face, your support, time, solidarity, and love mean a ton to us all.

Also, know that we're fighting from the inside just as vigorously as you are from the outside. And as a now fool said when he was once wise, "The revolution shall be televised." (They always said I should be a poet. LOL!)

But let me get back to the real. My name is Derick L. Forney . I am a Delaware prisoner currently being held captive in Pennsylvania's SCI-Coal Township (SCI-COA).

At the present time, the central office has approved me and most of the Vaughn17 prisoners to be placed on the RRL. This indefinite status is located in the RHU—the hole!

So, basically, we're to be locked down indefinitely in the hole. I've been housed in the RHU going on 190 days, today is 11-14-19. I'm still being punished for a crime I did not commit.

All of Vaughn17 is, being Delaware has acted maliciously by sending us to facilities in the PA/D.O.C so that we'd be further oppressed.

This is an act of double jeopardy. Vaughn17 prisoners charged in the uprising at James T. Vaughn Correctional Center, Smyrna, Delaware who were exonerated on all charges are not being treated as such—innocent.

And the b/s is that not all of Vaughn17 who were transferred to PA is on the RRL. Yeah! Some b/s! In the RHU, prisoners are treated like animals.

There is no system of order back here. The staff goes rogue, the meals are skimped and served cold, and there's no curriculum.

Instead, we're warehoused in cells with very little to do. There's no rehabilitation involved with the RHU/RRL unless one develops his own. And for those on the RRL, they have it the worst.

We are absolutely stuck with no time as to when we will be let go. There is no systemic design for RRL prisoners to take advantage of. Nothing for us to look forward to. Nothing for us to do. Little to no hope.

The education system is very biased. Teachers and the board of education here at SCI-COA has petitioned and grieved that they don't want to teach prisoners in the RHU. They don't want to have to travel back here just to teach us. And unless you're 21 and under, you will not receive an education on the RRL. And it is such a shame to hear that educators are protesting in order to not educate a certain group of prisoners.

The only program for prisoners on the RRL is a Step-Down Program which can only be recommended by the PRC team. And then the Central Office, specifically the Secretary of Corrections, John E. Wetzel, and the Executive Deputy Secretary, Tabb Bickell, will decide and make the final approval or denial on recommendations related to the RRL.

So, basically, these two figures are responsible for all prisoners who are on the RRL. According to the policy statement for the PA-DOC (commonwealth), under the DC-ADM 802 (Administrative Custody (AC) Procedures Policy), Section 1, (Placement on Administrative Custody (AC) status, paragraph C 1 and 2, there is a criterion that states what one should meet in order to be placed on the RRL. Paragraph C is the Restricted Release List (RRL) Placement "Procedure."

Now, this is where the b/s gets heavy because the AC status is correlated to the RRL status. A prisoner cannot grieve the RRL status, only the "long-term" AC status.

This loophole is created in order to trick prisoners into grieving a non-grieveable situation. This supports the fact that ambiguous standards exist. So if I try to grieve the RRL instead of the AC, my grievance will be denied as non-grieveable, and I will be time-barred. Also, none of the Vaughn17 prisoners meet the criteria.

We've never done PA time nor have we violated any policy rule or displayed any actions in PA that support this status of RRL. But due to the matter back in Delaware.

We are treated as atypical. And DE/DOC seems to be the center of our hardship.

PRC (Program Review Committee), the warden, the deputy warden are all aware of the fact that Delaware's D.O.C./personnel is in the middle of this.

Mental Health is aware, even regular guards are aware. The PRC team is nothing but a gang of brown-nosers who will lie to you like it's the truth.

They will spin you just to keep you off balance, to keep you calm, to mislead you, but keep you in the dark. The standards, the protocol, the procedures, the rules, the chain of command(s), everything!

It is ambiguous, misleading and at times, confidential. And the confidential policies open doors that enable PA-DOC to create loopholes to satisfy their illegal activities.

The Vaughn17 prisoners, as well as other prisoners, housed in the RHU and on RRL, are subjects who are being subjected to the vilest and inhumane treatment.

The Central Office has given some of the SCI's superintendents the discretion to run their prison in some unique ways. Arbitrary behavior is the main ingredient in this bowl of dysfunction.

I'm including with this letter an RHU handbook written by superintendent T. McGinley. It is the handbook for the RHU here at SCI-COA. It is a contradiction to the PA-DOC handbook briefly. I've requested the handbook multiple times. I am still without it.

They won't give me one because they know once I possess this jewel, I'll have the key to unlock the doors to revelation. And some of their loopholes will be ineffective. This handbook for the RHU at SCI-Coal Township allows the staff/guards to violate prisoners' rights. The handbook gives c/o's, sergeants, lieutenants, and other personnel the ability to take recreation (rec), showers, food, and whatever they deem an activity.

They use the 6:15 am count as a way to determine who gets these rights (but they consider these rights a privilege). If you are still in bed, or if your cell light is out, or if your bed isn't made or if you aren't dressed according to the guard's standards, you will not get your rec (yard), showers, razors (to shave), cell cleaning, even food is used as a punishment.

6:15 am is the most vulnerable time of the day for prisoners. We are either still asleep or just still in bed. And the counts are supposed to be announced via the PA system (loudspeaker). But it isn't.

Never do they call count time over the PA system in the mornings. And throughout the day, the count is called "some times." This is a practice that, because of how the RHU handbook is languaged, allows guards to burn prisoners for the following: showers, yard (rec), cell cleaning, razors (shave), and meals.

You see, I can use the phone still, commissary, and visit as well even if I don't stand with the lights on, dressed, etc, during count. And no other count except the morning will cause RHU/RRL prisoners to lose their rights. If there's something out front of the cell door that's in my area, I can lose all activities for the day.

Activities can be the mentioned rights. Showers are not to exceed 72 hours without one. And Mon-Fri rec is done for the standard of 1 hour. No movement in the RHU throughout the weekends. Showering every other day so when those pussies do the dumb shit and take what is a prisoner's right, a constitutional right, we are to go without showers, out-of-cell recreation, food, cleaning the cell, shaving...for days at a time. I've lost count of how many days I've gone hungry or without a proper hygiene opportunity. I can't even get my G.E.D. because they don't offer prisoners on the RLL or in the RHU education!

I am a Delaware prisoner along with the Vaughn17 prisoners who suffer because of something I had nothing to do with. Treated atypical and retaliated against, discriminatory conditions and inhumane treatment is what I live. Delaware has sent a message with us and PA/DOC is honoring the request.

Treat these individuals poorly. Violate their rights, their bodies, humiliate them, make their lives a living hell! And PA has yet to disappoint.

Most of the Vaughn17 prisoners are held in cells indefinitely for no valid reason. The conditions are beyond poor, below egregious, surpassing inhumane, unjust, and unconstitutional. It is blatant disrespect. We are shown the utmost prejudice and biased treatment. So it is up to you, the people, and us, the Vaughn17 prisoners and fellow comrades on RRL, to raise awareness. To raise a fist and fight the powers that be. Because we're the true power—the people. And we will not be overpowered by any opposing power. We will stand up. We will expose these pussies, expose their illegal activities. I thank you all for your ears. I pray that you all continue to be safe and suckafree. God bless you and yours. Peace. In the name of Solidarity, Strength, Resistance, and Resilience. Blessings and Love

Abednego Baynes

We have set out on a very specific mission to enhance the level of social awareness and unity in not only America but abroad. The Philosophy behind our course of action is the best way to help yourself is to first help others and don't ask of anyone what we don't ask of ourselves.

At this time we are looking at ways to better serve the communities that we have a presence in. We are also looking to build and unite resources to accomplish these goals. We can not refer to ourselves as a non-profit because we gain the same way that all those who participate do and that's by the building of unity, culture, and the passing of knowledge and wisdom.

We have to reconstruct our approach to problem-solving and make a deep logical assessment of where we are today and what is our best course of action to change tomorrow. All we are asking is that you aid us in aiding you.

It's not about where you came from or where you are at now, it's about taking what you have learned from point A (where you started) to point B (where you are at today) putting them forward, and making a change not only for others but also yourself. You can and will get out your environment and self what you put in it.

One person's problems ignored is sure to one day become our own. there is no mission that is impossible because a people united is unstoppable. You may see plenty of things on this website telling you who we are.

Our actions show how much we desire meaningful change not only for ourselves but for all those who are willing to accept it and the price we are willing to pay for it, but like I said to help others will always help you in return and that's the reason we stand here today seeking to further unite and make a real positive difference. We believe in our methods and practice only strengthen them, so we ask that you support us in supporting you, the people. Abednego Baynes

Pedro Chairez

"My name is Pedro Chairez, and I am one of the V-17 comrades who was publicly persecuted, vindictively indicted, and quietly exonerated. All at the hands of a corrupt and incompetent justice system. But the injustice, abuse, and oppression that preceded that monumental event and saturated every facet of our arrest, still lingers on…as our new captors enforce their own brand of internal retribution.

Passed around like cheap liquor we were shipped off to different states with a wink and a nod. The meaning clear: teach these boys a lesson!

We may have been exonerated in a court of law, but as far as prison officials go, we are guilty as hell. Like the stigmata, we will forever be stained with labels such as; instigators, trouble-makers, agitators, ring-leaders, gang-members, etc.

I was banished from my home state of Arizona and exiled to a foreign land, thousands of miles away from my family and friends. Not for my safety or better living conditions or rehabilitation. Nothing so magnanimous. It was purely punitive.

It is a tool and instrument to inflict psychological harm. They want to break down one's mental fortitude, sever him from his foundational support, weaken his resolve, silence his voice and crush his spirits. "Why," you ask? Simple. To make one more pliable and obedient.

Now I reside in Pontiac, Illinois. At their most restrictive and isolated prison facility. I am currently in Administrative Detention. A nice way of saying solitary confinement or segregation.

Here, I am warehoused like you would food products in a pantry. There are no programs, jobs, schools, or any other meaningful treatment available. No contact visits, chow halls, or religious groups. I live in a windowless cell, five feet wide and ten feet deep.

With a tv to pacify me and a fan for the summer. Furthermore, there's no legal justification for placing me here. Because my institutional behavior and 10yr sentence qualify for my minimum custody status.

However, when one challenges their procedures and reasoning, we get the intentionally vague and overused catch-phrase "institutional security". Which means everything and absolutely nothing. They know the courts are disinclined to intrude upon prison security matters. It is an unassailable position.

Equally important is that once we are entombed within these gulags, under the false pretense of being a security threat, they offer no viable means to work our way out of segregation.

There are no rehab programs, step-down programs, or "corrective" measures in place to help us transition back into the general population. We are in penitentiary purgatory. Stuck. There are people who have been in here for decades.

Without any tickets or gang activity. Yet we are continually denied release without rhyme or reason. For some it becomes hopeless. Suicide and serious mental illness are at an all-time high.

The purpose of explaining all this is because these are the same oppressive and draconian conditions that plague the prison systems across the nation, and which gave to the V-17 movement.

When you dehumanize people long enough they have a tendency to become inhumane. The government has marginalized and abandoned our Constitutional Rights. But the 8th Amendment is based on the fundamental premise that prisoners are not to be treated as less than human.

It is a right animated by broad and idealistic concepts of dignity, civilized standards, humanity, and decency. Something our congressional representatives have failed to uphold. But we have not. Nor will we bow down or cower under the weight of oppression. But I ask myself…why does violence have to erupt before it garners national attention? Why does tragedy have to precede accountability? Why is change so intimately linked to pain? Why is transparency so heavily shrouded in darkness? Why do we have to lose (fallen friends or buried alive) to win? I wish I had the answers, but I know why its called a struggle. Pedro Chairez

Dwayne Staats

Throughout ancient and modern times, there's been acts of rebellions, uprisings and insurrections orchestrated by valiant souls for the sake of a greater good.

Unfortunately, a lot of these events were either erased or distorted by the writers of history. This reality is why it's of the utmost importance for us to preserve the Vaughn17 saga and any other narratives that capture the same spirit of sacrifice, liberty, resistance and greater good as the martyrs that came before us.

One of the most renowned representations of such is Harriet Tubman. She not only liberated herself from the jurisdiction of slavery but on numerous occasions jeopardized her life and freedom to rescue thousands of others.

When the mind morphs into a by any means mode, the level of threat to the overall objective is what dictates the necessary. At times Harriet had to execute the fainthearted who denied themselves salvation to remain on the plantation. T

Hey were eliminated because in that instant they'd become a liability. It was too much at stake to take a chance on them not compromising or sabotaging the mission. In her eyes, she'd make sure they were freed one way or another....Nat Turner is another notable who marshaled one of the more militant rebellions that slaves themselves organized against oppression.

Their fight was to ensure everyone's freedom and dismantle the whole plantation and political system. Nat made practicable the element of surprise. He patiently waited while contemporaneously coordinating a clandestine ambush.

For them, an insurrection was the gateway to emancipation. Though less publicized than the others. Denmark Vesey spearheaded one of the most "boldly conceptualized" uprisings that ever materialized.

Sadly his demise came by the hands of house niggers and informants. Denmark was sentenced to death because of the audaciousness of his ambitions. The judge was so desensitized to the disenfranchisement haunting the slaves' existence, that the immensity of Denmark's sacrifice was unfathomable.

This was conveyed when he dumbfoundedly stated, "What infatuation could have prompted you to attempt an enterprise so wild and visionary. You were a free man, comely, wealthy and enjoyed every comfort compatible with your situation. You had, therefore, much to lose and little to gain.

Is slavery, then, a thing so detestable, that a man favored will engage in a plan that desperate merely to rescue his children from it?!" POWER IS THE PEOPLE!

Printed in the USA
CPSIA information can be obtained
at www.ICGtesting.com
LVHW020240060524
779442LV00030B/765